"I hear people often talk ab desert, or perceiving manna in the midst of broken seasons. But what does that mean? And how do we connect our heads, our hearts, and our souls with our seasons? I'm thankful for the careful shepherding of Meredith McDaniel. I'm thankful this book is in the kingdom, and I know you will be too."

JESS CONNOLLY, Bible teacher and author of *You Are the Girl for the Job*

"Meredith McDaniel, in writing her first book, has accomplished more than I was prepared for. In an effort to free us from the race we are all running, she focuses part of her work on the biblical understanding of divinely supplied spiritual nourishment that we as Christians call manna. God's faithfulness is unexpected but consistent, and I've not read anyone in a long time who explains that with such simple depth."

SUZANNE STABILE, author of *The Path Between Us*; coauthor of *The Road Back to You*

"With honesty and depth, Meredith invites us all to stop ignoring the pain of living in a broken world. She walks with us as we look directly into the depths of that pain in order to see God's hand already at work in the narrative of our lives. Without sugarcoating any of the brokenness, she offers hope—pure and powerful hope! God's love is bursting through the darkness! As you read, you may find yourself trading in your yearning for the next 'quick fix' for something more real and more satisfying. If you are looking for a light and fun read, look elsewhere. But if you are looking for something that is authentic, nourishing, and redemptive—you are right where you need to be."

ELLIE HOLCOMB, Dove Award–winning singer-songwriter

"The hunger for more seems to be part of the human condition. With the insightful care of a counselor, Meredith guides us to the answer our spirits desperately want to believe—that God is providing just what we need. *In Want + Plenty* invites you to come alive to the kind works of God in your everyday."

HAYLEY MORGAN, author of *Preach to Yourself*;
coauthor of *Wild and Free*
and *Always Enough, Never Too Much*

"Mining your own story is difficult, life-changing work, and Meredith's guidance through that process is gentle of spirit and fierce in truth."

KENDRA ADACHI, author of *The Lazy Genius Way*

"*In Want + Plenty* is a hauntingly beautiful and creative book offering priceless hope and reassurance to those of us who want more and are desperately searching to find it. Meredith's engaging style felt like we were having a conversation and re-awakened me to patterns of fear and anxiety that occur in my life when losses and disappointments dim my view of God's impressive strength, unfathomable wisdom, and endless love. In *Want + Plenty* is a house of gold; read it slowly and let it guide you to its treasures."

FIL ANDERSON, author of *Running on Empty*;
coauthor of *Blind Spots: What You Don't See
Can Hurt You*

"*In Want + Plenty* is a book that will touch the deep recesses of your heart, where you get thirsty and hungry for truth that nourishes and for our great God to meet you. This book can take you there. McDaniel courageously explores this territory, and you can follow on the path with her as your trusted guide. I recommend you grab a cup of coffee, put your feet up, and enjoy!"

"I don't believe Meredith McDaniel has ever been afraid to go deep, and this book is no exception. In *Want + Plenty* walks us humbly alongside an entire nation discovering and forgetting and rediscovering the sometimes uncomfortable but rich truths of God's provision, encouraging us to see with new eyes the gifts lying in wait all around us. Even in the hard stuff. Especially in the hard stuff. And it's beautiful. Quite true to herself, McDaniel acknowledges the ache is real while not allowing the reader to forget that the manna is real too . . . even if it doesn't look quite like we thought it would!"

"If you feel like you are walking alone in the desert (and even if you don't), let Meredith point you to the Creator who longs to be your guide. Sit down with her and embark on a treasure hunt for God's manna in your life. You will be glad you did!"

"I was struck by how eloquently Meredith peeled back the layers of my heart through Scripture and storytelling. Using her profession as a counselor, she weaves vulnerability with profound questions to draw the reader into deeper knowledge of self and God. If you are craving intimacy with Christ and others, these pages will whisper wisdom into your soul."

ANJULI PASCHALL, author of *Stay: Discovering Grace, Freedom, and Wholeness Where You Never Imagined Looking*; founder of The Moms We Love Club

"*In Want + Plenty* insists on providing hospitable space to explore and ask questions of God, ourselves, and each other. As a leader in the local church, I'm aware of the need for honest and healthy conversations around traditionally private matters like longing and discontentment, and I believe addressing that need is critical to the welfare of our personal and corporate relationships with God. Meredith McDaniel gives ample opportunity to delve deeper, listen longer, and trust more fully. What a generous gift to us!"

GREG LAFOLLETTE, artist and spiritual director; director of arts and liturgy, Grace Story Church, Nashville, Tennessee

"We all know that our world is full of hurting people. What we may be hesitant to admit is that those of us who file into churches each weekend also carry brokenness that can be soul crushing, leaving us numb and disillusioned. Meredith writes like a good friend speaking to you over coffee and saying, 'It's OK to not be OK!' As you read *In Want + Plenty*, suddenly you find yourself believing that God desperately wants more for us, and that he is standing before us offering healing and real life. Oh friend, Meredith offers hope and freedom in these pages!"

HOLLY WORSLEY, community builder and gospel storyteller

in want + plenty

WAKING UP TO GOD'S PROVISION IN A LAND OF LONGING

MEREDITH MCDANIEL

Revell

a division of Baker Publishing Grou
Grand Rapids, Michigan

Published by Revell
a division of Baker Publishing Group
PO Box 6287, Grand Rapids, MI 49516-6287
www.revellbooks.com

Printed in the United States of America

Library of Congress Cataloging-in-Publication Data
Names: McDaniel, Meredith, 1983– author.
Title: In want + plenty : waking up to God's provision in a land of longing / Meredith McDaniel.
Other titles: In want and plenty
Description: Grand Rapids : Revell, a division of Baker Publishing Group, 2020.
Identifiers: LCCN 2019036303 | ISBN 9780800735791 (paperback)
Subjects: LCSH: Providence and government of God—Christianity. | Desire—Religious aspects—Christianity. | Moses (Biblical leader) | Bible. Exodus, XX—Criticism, interpretation, etc. | Storytelling—Religious aspects—Christianity.
Classification: LCC BT135 .M325 2020 | DDC 248.8/43—dc23
LC record available at https://lccn.loc.gov/2019036303

the people and situations described in this
or presented in composite form in order
those with whom the author has worked.

am Overbeeke
Guthe of True Cotton Art

25 26   7 6 5 4 3 2 1

In memory of my beloved mentor

Bobbi Aker Campbell

June 6, 1946–May 21, 2018

+

for anyone else who, like Moses,
at times may feel like an alien in a foreign land

"If we find ourselves
with a desire that nothing
in this world can satisfy,
the most probable explanation
is that we were made
for another world."

—C. S. Lewis

contents

foreword

IT'S SUMMERTIME IN LONDON, and my family and I are visiting for the week, a trip we've been looking forward to for months. After a long day in the city, we head back to catch the train to our place in Windsor. The sun is still high at 7:00 p.m. as we cross on foot over the Golden Jubilee Bridge. We hear the small crowd before we see them gathered near the Millennium Wheel, and we walk up casually behind them to see what captures their attention.

What we see is a man standing in the center next to a small platform. From the size of the crowd and the excitement of the man, it seems as though he's building up to a grand finale. Thinking we walked up at just the right time, we decide to hang around and see what will happen next. Perhaps he has an unspeakable talent, maybe as a contortionist or a musician. What will he do? We soon find out.

First, he invites the people standing in front to step in a little closer, a little closer, one more step in. Good. Then he gets the crowd clapping together, slowly at first, then a little faster, until the clapping becomes so fast it all blurs together and sounds like applause. This, of course, draws even more passersby to join our skeptical group, all waiting for the man in the middle to do something worthy of the applause he's conjured.

By now a few minutes have passed and my husband's interest has waned. He's ready to continue our walk to the train station, but the kids and I hold out hope, knowing as soon as we walk away, that's when the good stuff will happen. Maybe he'll perform a remarkable feat, like breathe fire or turn backflips or do magic! Whatever is about to happen will certainly be awe-inspiring, the likes of which we'll be telling our families for years to come. *You'll never believe what we saw one summer in London,* we'll say. *It was unlike anything we've seen before or since.*

Of course that's not what happened. Instead, we hung around to watch this man bark orders to the crowd for the better part of fifteen minutes. While I expected this man to show off an impressive talent in music or gymnastics, he was displaying talent of a different kind. He gathered a crowd of interested strangers not because of something he could *do* but because of something he *knew*: we are wired to want to know what happens next.

Story is built into our bones and brains and DNA. It's what keeps us turning the page, watching the next episode, staying up late, leaning in closer . . . *and then what happened?* It's what compels us to stand with a group of strangers on a sidewalk next to the River Thames and watch a man attract a crowd with nothing but his loud voice and a knack for building anticipation. We only change the channel, put down the book, or walk away when we stop caring what happens next.

Stories shape us and they may also heal us. But they can't do either if we aren't willing to hear them or tell them. Our unwillingness (or inability) to face the stories our lives are telling will not keep those stories from speaking. It will simply keep us from having a say in the way they play out.

The Bible is the story of how God created the world and of what happened next. We may read it for information, but it won't bring transformation until we see how our story fits into it. And that's the gift Meredith McDaniel brings in the pages of this book. She doesn't merely point back to the story of how God rescued his people in history. She also points within, inviting us into the story of how God is rescuing us now and reminding us of his provision in the everyday manna he provides. This manna—a word literally translated from the Hebrew expression for "What is it?"—invites us to lean forward and listen for an explanation. God's provision doesn't always explain itself. Sometimes it shows up as a question and we ask *What is it? What does it mean? What now?* Meredith walks with us through all of those questions, inviting us to place our hope in our friend Jesus, who is our ultimate provision in both want and plenty.

Every generation needs kind companions who will teach us how to live, how to relate, and how to remember. Meredith is one of those companions, and it's with a grateful heart I usher you into the pages of this book. I wonder what will happen next?

Emily P. Freeman
Author of *The Next Right Thing*

lay of the land

A guide to elements and visuals
of *In Want + Plenty*

manna

man·na | \ 'ma-nə \

a. food miraculously supplied to the Israelites in their
   journey through the wilderness

b. divinely supplied spiritual nourishment

c. a usually sudden and unexpected source of gratifica-
   tion, pleasure, or gain

»re:vision

the shifting of one's lens in life, especially in the light of further evidence

Look Back (past)
foundation + self-identity

Be Still (current)
owning struggle + listening

Scan Horizon (future)
fear/hope + movement

---

re:story

the experiential process of rewriting one's story line through re:Vision

---

re:sound

the intentional act of slowing down to listen to music that helps heal

life in the ebb + flow

In this life we await what is to come—
we ache, we laugh, we love, we live
Yearning for the already / not yet and glimpsing
of the goodness right in our midst

We flail when storms brew—doubting,
grasping for a Hope that will satisfy
The clouds darken, the rain rhythms, then
soaks, and all we want is relief

We birth, breathe, celebrate, grieve, create,
and yet spend our lives longing for more
If we could just hold in our hand what we think
we need, we say, then maybe, peace?

Moment by moment we find ourselves
feasting or falling, reveling or revealing
We try to hold it all together, forgetting that
we have a God who holds us in his hand

We try to cling to what we know is true,
seeking refuge as the cruel waves crash
Getting lost in a game of performance and
appearance, we hide our deep and dark

In our struggle we lose sight of the glory; in
our story we must hunt for his hand
We look in every place here on this broken
earth, when contentment is found Beyond

So we ponder how we can let the Current
carry us when life unfolds unexpectedly
When we unravel in our raw reflections of a
God who claims he is close by, even in this

We are *manna makers*: doctors, neighbors, lovers,
mothers, fathers, sons, and daughters
Living our everyday in the messy and mundane,
chaotic and clumsy controlled corners

Full life, the kind we all keep trying to unearth,
is found right here, in the ebb and flow

"As the mind explores the symbol, it is led to ideas that lie beyond the grasp of reason."

—Carl Jung

prologue

And he rained down on them manna to eat
and gave them the grain of heaven.
Man ate of the bread of the angels;
he sent them food in abundance. . . .
And they ate and were well filled.

Psalm 78:24–25, 29 ESV

I'M SITTING HERE silently gazing out the window, watching the birds in my yard dancing wildly in the sunshine, uninhibited. They appear to have an understanding with our Creator that they will be given *enough* for today. Don't you envy that kind of certainty?

I long to be like the birds who "do not sow or reap or store away in barns" (Matt. 6:26). Yet I endlessly hustle and gather in an effort to satisfy my thirst and hunger. I wonder what our bodies, minds, and souls would be like if we all could live in such sweet surrender?

I'm flooded with story upon story of women, students, and families who have walked into my counseling office and feel like they *have had enough and they are not enough.* They want more from life but don't know where to find it. They've tried everything, followed the formulas, yet most things are not panning out the way they planned, and they are left wanting more. As a counselor, I am well acquainted with the narratives of a wide variety of people. I have seen firsthand the healing power of Narrative Therapy in my practice over the past fifteen years. Taking the time to look back, name where we are currently, and look ahead not only helps us reclaim our identity and true self but also provides us space to shift and move as life happens, so we can ride the wave with it.

We tell ourselves we want the best out of life and for those we love. We attend school for years and seek jobs that provide money to pay the bills and get what we want. We travel, indulge in food, and shop until we drop. We collect and create. We meditate and exercise. We go to therapy and maybe even attend church. We read self-help books, blogs, and magazines to enhance every portion of our being. We are constantly consuming content that makes our mind spin and causes us to compare ourselves to others. *We inevitably forget who we are and what we were made for.*

We tend to walk around with a false script in the back of our minds, whispering lies that if we can just work hard enough, life will go the way we want and we will be happy. Yet it doesn't take long for us to realize life doesn't work that way. No matter how hard we try and no matter how much we attain, an ache remains. Life happens and we realize we are not in control.

Recently I sat with a young woman in her early thirties named Veda. She slumped onto my vintage couch in her cozy yoga pants after a long morning of juggling her life. Taking a deep breath, she looked up at me with weary eyes, as if she might be more content just lying down and taking a nap for the next hour rather than talking about her problems. She was *exhausted.* Veda is a mother to four, wife to her high school sweetheart, and overwhelmed by her current season of life. She was quick to tell me her love for her family and her desire to love them better, yet her primary reason for coming to counseling was to figure out why she could not seem to fully connect with the people in her life. She recently had become aware, on a soul level, of a *disconnect* with her close friends and family. Veda described the feeling as a wall shooting up in her heart when she starts to feel vulnerable. Even in positive intimacy with someone, the wall remains. Over time she began to share how she had buried her own pain, and even her dreams and desires, in an effort to emotionally survive her lonely lifestyle. With tears in her eyes, she was at a loss for how to fix things, and she couldn't put her finger on how she ended up there.

We all feel this to some degree. We have high hopes for our life, and then we wake up and realize life looks different from what we had in mind. We battle and cope with the brokenness of the world in our own ways based on our personality, patterns, and the lens through which we see the world. Using the model of the Enneagram, authors Ian Cron and Suzanne Stabile have wisely explained this paradigm we operate under: "Human beings are wired for survival. As little kids we instinctually place a mask called personality over parts of our authentic self to protect us from harm and to make our way in the world."[1]

The Enneagram is a nine-point symbol that represents nine distinct strategies for relating to ourselves, others, and the world.[2] It reveals that we all have a history and carry around a backpack full of all our junk. At some point we might start to blame ourselves for the way life has ended up. We think, *If I had just done this differently, maybe I wouldn't be in this mess.* Sometimes we blame others for the heartache we feel, and other times we blame God. Many days the blame is scattered among all three.

Having a mind-set of blame could lead to a very bleak outcome. The unfortunate truth is that many of us walk around every day with an inability to put these emotions into words, and we either feel like a failure or like the world has failed us. When all our efforts leave us wanting, we tend to grow depressed and anxious, and then we begin to unravel. We can't hold it together anymore, and we become paralyzed. We disconnect from others and isolate. The last thing we tend to do is reach out for the support of our community or reveal how we feel.

But what if we took some time to discover more and look deeper into our story?

Hope for the Weary

What if we gazed up at our Maker, locked eyes with him, and trusted that what he has in store for us and our people is actually *best*? What if we believed that he is already providing for us nonstop, even in the midst of our chaotic circumstances that make no logical sense to us? Even when we don't think he sees us or cares, what if we were able to rest in the remembering of his goodness?

What if that perspective might relieve us of all the unnecessary pressure we put on ourselves to live a certain way and strive so hard to make things happen the way we want?

But is it that easy?

I don't know about you, but I want to love who God created me to be and know that I was not an accident but that a well-meaning, intentional Creator handcrafted every gift and quirk of my being.

I want to find calm in the chaos of every season and live freely and confidently in who I am.

I want to feel richly connected to friends and family and strangers alike, with a profound knowing that we are all in this broken world together.

Recognizing that we were made for something more, I want to be deeply rooted with a firm foundation I can stand on no matter what storm comes my way.

I want to be compelled to look beyond myself and love others out of an overflow that simply cannot be contained.

I want to be known and loved just as I am and live out the purpose I was created for right now.

That kind of wholeness is what we were made for.

If I'm honest though, I understand that every day there seems to be something else that makes people want to give up and reject all they know to be true. Sometimes all it takes is getting news from a friend or family member. Maybe it's waking up and glimpsing the headlines that pop up on your phone. Or maybe it's lying awake at night wondering why you feel the way you do and how to make it better. A sense of entitlement envelops our soul, and we start to flail and scramble to create the life we have dreamed up on our own. I've been there.

Life is an ebb and flow. I ache for the men and women who come to my counseling office and entrust me with their thorns. My heart breaks when I sit on my porch with a hurting friend who feels like the rug has been pulled out from under her. Yet when I am exposed to other people's stories, the world starts to feel a little smaller and I realize that the ache is universal and beyond me. When I open the ancient text of the Bible and see it apply directly to our modern world, I stand in awe. God's *unmerited mercy* is threaded into every story line, and I see his provision pouring out every day in the lives of those I quietly sit with.

Part of reading this book is dipping your toes into some self-reflection on your personal story. You may or may not feel up to doing this on your own, and it is healthier to navigate with others.

Considering Your Own Story

There is a common story that ties us all together:

We want more, and we are desperately searching to find it.

I have discovered a consistent pattern of fear and anxiety unraveling souls amid the loss and disappointment that we experience when life is different than we expect. I have found that the longing persists, and the pain can be relentless when we become blind to the goodness right before us. Our aching trumps our ability to see and take hold of God's present provision, and it is as if a blindfold is placed on our eyes and hope evaporates. Oh, how we yearn.

If you feel as if you might fall apart if one more wave crashes over you in your life, this book is for you.

If you feel like you can't handle all the responsibilities placed upon your shoulders, this book is for you.

If you find yourself waking up anxious in the middle of the night because the list of things you have yet to do is clouding your tired mind, this book is for you.

If you are going through a transition from one season to the next and you feel as if you might break in the process, this book is for you.

If you feel like enough is enough and *you* are not enough to keep all the plates spinning, this book is for you!

The first place to begin gaining a new perspective is with your own personal story. Sometimes we have to look back before we can move forward and find healing. I won't pretend to know all the ins and outs of your life, as I understand everyone's family and life circumstances vary greatly. *You* are the true expert on all things you, so it will be essential to dig into your narrative as we go on this journey together.

Sometimes we have to look back before we can move forward and find healing.

Throughout the book we will take time to pause and journal what comes to mind in your own story. Research shows, and I have found this to be true, that taking intentional time to *listen* to what God is whispering and being *mindful* of his presence leads to inner healing. Opportunities to slowly process your story will be interlaced throughout the book. So grab some paper and a pen to accompany you on this journey, or purchase the companion narrative journal to keep nearby. These questions will guide you as you sit and write all that has been stirred in your heart and will help you trace the hand of our God in your story with fresh eyes. So let's take a few moments right now to practice this spiritual discipline of *waking up*. Think about the big things that stand out in your life as you survey the past few decades and trace it all back.

Let's begin laying the foundation with the following Back to Basics questions:

> » How were you raised?
>
> » What did your daily family dynamics look like?
>
> » What did you love when you were little?
>
> » What memories do you have from grade school?
>
> » What were your greatest disappointments in middle/high school?
>
> » What has broken your heart?
>
> » What makes you come alive currently?

By taking some time to remember as both happy and hard things come to mind, we start to uncover the parts of ourselves that have been buried inside us. We begin to connect the dots and discover why we feel and act the way we do now because of what happened years ago. Digging up the past can be a brutal process that many of us are not eager to engage in, but it is worth it.

I had the bittersweet gift of beginning this process myself in a counseling office during college, and it sparked an abundant journey of healing in my life that I do not anticipate ceasing on this side of heaven. It is a gift of constant refinement. I knew I wanted more from my life and desired to live out the purpose I was created for, but I was at a loss for how to get there. I needed someone to take my hand, guide me through my story, and help me reclaim my true identity. I needed to find a way to *wake up* to my life with fresh eyes.

In his book *To Be Told*, Dan Allender writes about coauthoring our stories with God: "So take seriously the story God has given you to live. It's time to read your own life because your story is one that could set us all ablaze."[3]

My counselor serves as an unbiased third party and helps to gently guide me through all my mess. I've gained invaluable insight that has transformed my life and helped to break cycles and patterns I was enslaved by for many years. Today, I create this safe space for my own counseling clients in hopes of walking with them through the heavy so that they might feel even a little lighter.

I hope that by entering the narrative journey together in this book you will gain similar insight into the burning in your own heart and the ache of your own story. I pray that through looking back *you will be able to unearth the provision* you might not naturally see.

You Are Not Alone

Our Creator wants nothing more than to be part of this process with us, and he is simply inviting *you* to take the time to ponder all he has done along the way and is currently doing in your life.

I have walked through a variety of heavy seasons with people battling intense longings and disappointments. Yet I'm blown away every time as I watch people find an *indescrib-able peace* and *light in the dark*. When I hear what has happened to people, I have at times found myself questioning the goodness of God. Questions and doubts still rise up in me after many years of practice. But it doesn't take long to see the beauty that is birthed from brokenness when people allow God to enter in and restore their hearts. He is a good God and is always near. This is truth, even on the hardest of days.

You may hear that and feel like it might be true for some people but not for you. I don't want to pretend that I know what you are walking through, because I don't. What I *do* know is that the words of the Bible are alive and true. The promises and stories that unfold through the Old and New Testaments are just that—a testament to God's provision in the midst of the hardest circumstances time and time again.

I wonder what God is up to in your life. What light is trying to crack through in the darkest parts of your story and heart?

A Lifelong Journey

I want you to know that I am not just inviting you to look deeper into your story; I will also be delving deeper into my own story through our time together. *It is a lifelong journey.* It is not like we reach some level of self-discovery and then cease the soul-searching and chasing after God. The truth is, the more we find out, the more we realize how little we know. We get a taste of the mystery of God and long to know more. We start to see the patterns that persist in our life and we want to change to become more like Jesus and who he created us to be.

For the bulk of my life I believed that to be in God's "good graces" we were required, as his people, to be obedient and to pretend like we had it all together. It never crossed my mind that we are allowed to be sad in the longing, much less to expose our pain.

We innocently use verses like Romans 8:28 ("And we know that in all things God works for the good of those who love him") as ammo to fuel our hardworking mentality. Many days we go through life denying that there is a deeper problem beneath the surface. We tend to suppress the loud longing and live blissfully ignorant within the rat race of our jobs, schools, and families.

The ache is rooted in the reality that no matter how hard we try, we cannot provide the solution to our problem. We simply cannot work hard enough to ease the pain we feel. The truth is that we are not enough; we need Someone greater than us to rescue us and do what only he can do.

Every person who has breathed in the dense air of this broken world has felt this *ache*. It is easier to see the pain in others who desire more from this life; but when it comes to looking at our *own* pain, we tend to distract ourselves and grow numb.

It's like an unrelenting toothache that we can only ignore for so long before getting it repaired.

A Narrative Journey: Looking Back to Move Ahead

By looking back into ancient history and the early days of God's people, I hope that we might enter a narrative journey to discover God's provision in even the hardest of circumstances. That we might allow the stories of those who have gone before us to unravel our own narratives. That we would come out on the other side with fresh eyes to *see*.

I long for us all to wake up to the full life God created for us to live.

The words of Scripture and a persistent stirring in my soul often remind me that *we were made for more than this.* We were made for more than this inability to enjoy the moment and the gifts right before us due to our stubborn focus on what is missing.

As I think back to the garden of Eden and imagine the beauty and freedom Adam and Eve experienced before brokenness entered our world, I am jealous. They glimpsed God's glory! Can you picture a world without pain or suffering? Or a world without the need to hide? Pause there for a second and really envision what that would be like. It's hard to wrap our mind around a world like that, isn't it? What we see today is the brokenness of an overgrown garden as vines entangle and choke out the life of God's greatest creation—us.

Every day we tend to fall into living out of our false self, a cheapened version of God's best for us.

Every day we tend to fall into living out of our false self, a cheapened version of God's best for us. We think we know best, and when life surprises us we grow bitter. When we don't get what we want, we flail and indulge in what we know brings only a temporary fix to ease our pain.

Through each loss we are forced to face the reality that we are all given one fleeting life here on earth. We can fall prey to the paralysis of anxiety and depression, or we can cling to the hope that during all the grief and longing we will be met right where we are by a God who loves us and aches alongside us.

On any given day I teeter somewhere between those extremes. Yet every time I am faced with the reality of the grave, something rises up within me. I am reminded of how we were made to experience more here on earth and beyond this earth. Something about the richness of life in these moments when we feel as if we might break brings forth a window into full life. Our earthly longings begin to fade when we realize how precious life itself is.

We simply cannot fill the hole in our hearts that we are born with, no matter how hard we try. We look around at what others have and feel a sense of entitlement—we should have that too. And it isn't just stuff that we want; many times we simply want to acquire deeper relationships and community. We have friends, but they may only glimpse what inhabits our hearts. We find ourselves dating or marrying another broken person, and our combined broken patterns break us apart. We end up feeling alone and isolated, when our deepest need is for intimacy. This disconnection drives us to our worst habits. We let the darkness begin to overtake the light in our own mind and heart.

No matter what our hopes, dreams, or goals in life, there comes a time when we feel overlooked or forgotten. Toddlers grab toys from friends' hands, elementary kids trade cards on the playground to build their collection, middle schoolers conform in groups to feel like they belong, and high schoolers compete to get into college. College students elbow their way up to the top jobs, working adults climb the ladder in their careers, and families obtain all the basics and beyond to have the perfect American household image. Once we get *all the things*, we soon become enticed by the next trendy item on our Amazon wish list. But our budget may be small, which breeds bitterness and anger over what we cannot afford. We get grabby and our soul dries up, and it affects everything. We can't sleep because our mind races with the next day's to-do list. We work overtime and break under the stress and pressure of our job. We avoid people to hide the pain we feel, and we enter dark places and believe lies that dampen our dreams.

When we stop feeling, dreaming, and longing, we give in to the false belief that our Creator is holding out on us. We don't allow ourselves to feel the emotions that flow as a result of our distrust, and we are unable to connect with people or God. We guard our heart and keep those we love at bay to resist the pain that may come. We feel unworthy of loving well and accepting love.

> » Where do you see yourself doing this in your own life?
>
> » Do you want to feel this way forever?
>
> » Do you believe there is a way to find peace in all this?
>
> » Do you really buy the truth that you were made for more?

Manna

We are not alone in this yearning for life to look and feel different. Even Paul, an apostle of Jesus, felt this tug to make sense of our world: "I consider that our present sufferings are not worth comparing with the glory that will be revealed in us"

(Rom. 8:18). By taking a long look back at Moses leading the Israelites in their Exodus journey, we can wake up, regain our sight, and see clearly once more. We realize that thousands of years ago the Israelites were asking the same questions that we still ask today.

When will I be relieved of my aching? How long will I groan? Can I really trust God?

My hope is that by using the book of Exodus as our guide, we will travel together on a narrative journey—a quest if you will—to trace the hand of our Creator throughout a 440-plus-year wilderness. Along the way we will be reminded that just as God met every need of his people then, he does so for us today. God promised, "So I have come down to rescue them from the hand of the Egyptians and to bring them up out of that land into a good and spacious land, a land flowing with milk and honey" (Exod. 3:8). We all long to live once again in the bliss of garden-like innocence with all its abundance, yet we each await heaven in this in-between space called Earth, craving what is still to come.

Meanwhile, in the desert places God says, "I will rain down bread from heaven for you. The people are to go out each day and gather enough for that day" (Exod. 16:4). The Israelites named this bread of the wilderness *manna*, which came in the form of small round flakes that were found on the ground like morning dew. The Hebrew *man hu* means "What is it?" since the Israelites were in awe of this gift of grace but didn't know what it was or the value it held.[4] They were desperate for nourishment, but when God provided it, they had many doubts and questions.

Manna reveals the intentional love of our Creator, who uniquely tailors provision for his people out of his deep knowing of our personalities. Manna is a smile from a stranger. Manna is a child catching fireflies. Manna is a salty breeze. Manna is a check in the mail. Manna is God's love.

Manna stuns us in our steps. Manna reminds us that God is near, no matter what is happening around us. Manna prompts us to see the reality that God loves us and can be trusted, even when our circumstances or the state of our heart may beg to differ. When we are ready to throw in the towel and say enough is enough, God gently extends grace in the form of manna and proves that he is indeed more than enough.

I believe that God fulfills his promises to his people, both in the dry, desert-wandering seasons and in the fruitful glimpses of heaven meeting earth. Life doesn't always look like what we might have had in mind, but I wonder if there is something in the manna he provided for Israel that might also apply to us today. We have a tendency to go through this land of longing bound by the fear and anxiety that come from loss and disappointment. Yet I have come to see that hope can be found in the ultimate Provider. By continuing to flip through these pages, you will uncover pain but also beauty. Exploring your story and our shared history will give you *hope*.

God fulfills his promises to his people, both in the dry, desert-wandering seasons and in the fruitful glimpses of heaven meeting earth.

Hang with me, and I can promise you that hope will begin to rise up to the surface for us all.

We will ask three types of *re:Vision* questions along the way. On the top of each page where you journal, ask these questions for each section of the book as together we *Look Back, Be Still,* and *Scan the Horizon*:

>> **Where was/is God who is supposed to hold it all together?**

>> **How can he be here in this when it hurts so much?**

>> **How can I trust and rest in him as I look ahead?**

Will you join me in discovering the hidden manna in your own life?

re:sound

"We Will Feast in the House of Zion"
by Sandra McCracken

deep groans

I AM MADE FOR MORE

We know that the whole creation has been groaning as in the pains of childbirth right up to the present time. . . . But if we hope for what we do not yet have, we wait for it patiently.

Romans 8:22, 25

"He that lacks time to mourn,
lacks time to mend."

—Sir Henry Taylor

one

MANY GENERATIONS had flowed from the family of Jacob since the time when Joseph was a ruler in the land of Egypt. As the baton of power passed to new pharaohs who did not remember Joseph, the Israelites went from being guests to slaves swept up by the king's desire for wealth. Thousands of Hebrew fathers, mothers, boys, and girls lived within magnificent cities being built by the daily labor of their hands.

So many Hebrew babies were being born, the pharaoh grew fearful of the Israelites' sheer numbers. Determined to preserve his power, he increased their workload in an effort to create an illusion of epic proportions. His earthly kingdom was shiny and outwardly impressive, gleaming in the sun with gold and grandeur. With ruthless eyes only on his prize, he worked the Israelite slaves mercilessly. And God's people just mindlessly kept putting one foot in front of the other to survive each day.

As the Israelite population continued to explode, however, the pharaoh took matters into his own bloody hands. He sent word that every newborn Hebrew boy must be thrown into the River Nile. But the Hebrew midwives disobeyed him, and the cries of the babies were still heard in Israelite homes.

One Hebrew mother placed her baby boy in a woven papyrus basket and prayed he would float to safety. Pharaoh's daughter found the floating bundle and sent her maid to fetch it. Her heart melted at the baby's first cry, which carried through the palace at the river's edge. She named the child Moses and found an Israelite woman, who happened to be his birth mother, to nurse him during his early years. Pharaoh's daughter eventually adopted Moses into the royal family, and he spent his formative years living among the Egyptians.

When Moses grew up, he saw the injustice his people faced under the pharaoh's rule. One day he saw an Egyptian strike a Hebrew slave, one of his true relatives, and in anger Moses killed the man and buried him in the sand. This act of rebellion forced him to flee.

Leaving behind everything he knew, Moses found himself by a well in the land of Midian, alone.

Waking up in the dark shadows of our bedroom, we fumble around for our phone where it rests on our nightstand. We crave connection and believe the illusion that our scrolling will suffice. The bright light beams into our brain as we open inboxes and gaze groggily at filtered faces, and our heart pounds at the blurred boxes of Instagram. We let the lies in.

They have what I don't. God is holding out on me. I will never be who I want to be. What if I feel this way forever?

We are blinded to the beauty right before us: the breath that we just took, the bed that we are lying in, and the roof over our head.

We want.

At any point on any given day we all yearn for something.

Love.

Home.

Community.

Rest.

Peace.

Contentment.

Whether it is a desire for something fleeting like chocolate or more permanent like our dream house, entitlement enslaves us and convinces us we need more. Living in a consumer culture and being bombarded by ads creatively embedded throughout our devices only fuels these cravings. Not only do we want tangible items from Amazon that we can hold in our hands within hours, but we also want to *feel* differently. We sense there is more to our story.

There is a deep desire to have our life under our control and appear like nothing negative truly affects us. The preference is to tie up loose ends with pretty bows and dress up in our Sunday best to hide the aching we feel. We cut off conversations with friends who try to take us places we are not ready to go. Disconnecting from how we really feel in the moment and trying to push back our emotions works at first. But like a buoy in the sea, those emotions bounce back up and wreak havoc in our heart. Compulsively, we bury the pain.

This happened to me just last week while I was having coffee with a friend. We had been planning to get together for months, and she is (thankfully) someone who asks me the hard questions before the froth has been sipped. She dropped hints the whole time, wanting to know how I was *really* feeling about balancing work and family. But every time she tried to go there I changed the subject to something easier.

We don't want to go there. *Just let me sip my latte and talk about nothing already, please.*

>> **What is popping up in your mind right now?**

>> **What areas do you avoid in your life?**

So we work hard. We run on adrenaline, moving quickly from one thing to the next so that we can ignore the unsettledness in our souls. We make to-do lists in our planners or bullet journals and think if we can just tick enough boxes in our day, then we might find contentment. The self-help section of our local bookstore will forever be bursting at the seams with topical playbooks filled with life hacks from the experts because we cannot get enough.

The fact that you are sitting here holding this book in your hands means you are probably looking for a formula or tools to help ease the pain your own life is causing right now. We skim through, highlighting words that might breathe some life into the daily heaviness we face. We want to escape from our own chaos and read about other people's lives for a hot minute. We don't really want to face the relationships or circumstances that are making us ache. So instead of slowing down to find the root of our struggles, we do the opposite. We start hustling through our days, then get up the next morning and do it all again. Numb.

What if our days started out differently? What if we took five minutes to sit before moving?

It can be unfamiliar and unnerving to sit still and put aside our agendas for the day, even for five minutes. Sitting still and feeling what might be stirring within us isn't usually at the top of our priority list. But what if it were? What if we lit a candle and listened quietly to what bubbles up to our soul's surface? I wonder what might come to mind and how our bodies might benefit from easing into the day like that. What if we stopped trying to read or write or even hear something from God? What if we sat still for five minutes with no plan and no purpose other than simply being and breathing? You might already be squirming just thinking about it.

>> What are you avoiding?

>> What is it that you can't sit with?

When we take time for stillness, we are choosing to let any underlying emotions rise to the surface. It can feel like a flood, and we may not be ready for it. When we turn off our phones (or launch them across the room) to focus on a book or a person, we find we aren't used to facing ourselves. We feel uncomfortable. It seems too quiet, and we reach for the phone again.

Can we talk about how maybe the best thing Apple has ever done is offering the Screen Time app on iPhones? The option to create a literal downtime has given me so much of my life back and reveals just how much time I had been wasting. No one can argue with a color-coded graph that breaks down our mindless scrolling on our handheld devices into every category from email to Instagram.

I wonder what immerses your mind as you enter the unfamiliar and haunting quiet of stillness. Take a moment to sit and be mindful of these questions. Consider what your body wants to do.

» Do you feel uneasy because you feel like you need to be doing something other than sitting?

» Does your to-do list take over and assist in numbing the feelings?

» Do you feel unsettled because when you are with other people you are able to deflect and ask them questions to avoid what is really going on in your mind?

Rest comes in the stillness of surrender, when we relax and realize we cannot hold it together. Opening our hands to what Jesus has for us in the moment versus what we think we need breeds peace. When we learn to live in abundance instead of scarcity, *a calm comes over us*. We can start to hear God whispering for us to lean on him and lay down all the thoughts that are swirling. We start to breathe again in the silence.

Rest comes in the stillness of surrender, when we relax and realize we cannot hold it together.

Yet many of us are proficient performers. We just keep moving at a pace we can't maintain. We are masterminds at making our own life appear better than it really is. We are selectively transparent around the few people who we allow ourselves to slow down enough to connect with, usually omitting the dark details. Eventually we give in to the illusion that by obtaining all the comforts of this world and by craftily numbing out, our own longings and desires will then be satisfied.

If I can just get my life in order . . .

If I can just find some friends who get me . . .

*If I can just spend more time making myself more whole . . .
Maybe then life would feel a little less stressful and I might
experience more peace.*

Sound the buzzer. Wrong!

Those deceptive thoughts leave us exhausted as we try to
attain the life we have always wanted and start "running on
empty," as author and spiritual director Fil Anderson calls it.[1]
We try to make it all happen on our own. We unravel under all
the pressure we pile on ourselves, and we grow complacent in
our discontentment. We interpret our failed plans as our own
fault, or we might even shift the blame onto those around us.
We are on edge, restless, and unhappy. We are out of control,
and we feel it deep in our bones.

Taking the time to be still uncovers what is beneath the
surface, which leads to the root of our ache.

We Are Slaves

You see, we have a covert enemy whispering lies into our heart
that we are not enough and we are not doing enough. The
enemy also craftily convinces us that our Creator is holding
out on us. He knows what causes you personally to doubt or
fear or hurt. He is fully aware of how to use your own history to fuel the lies and make them believable for you in your
context. We want a quick, easy, simple fix for what is broken;
we want it our way and in our time. We were made for a glorious garden overflowing with goodness and delight, but many
times we feel as if we are fumbling around in a wasteland that
grows darker daily. We struggle to find light.

C. S. Lewis wrote, "We can ignore even pleasure. But pain
insists upon being attended to. God whispers to us in our

pleasures, speaks in our conscience, but shouts in our pain: it is his megaphone to rouse a deaf world."[2] As I sit with women and men of all ages in my counseling office and hear the heaviness of each sacred story and the patterns of pain that persist, I cannot deny that brokenness abounds.

I hear people speak of strained relationships, burnout, rape, addiction, divorce, eating disorders, compulsions, identity loss, dissociating, perfectionism, illness, cutting, and abuse, to name just a few. I sit stunned at what the enemy has meant for evil in the most unimaginable circumstances. I honestly find myself wanting to wave a magic wand over those sitting before me and miraculously fix it all. This is not possible, however; it is not my job nor is it the answer to the problems. My job looks more like entering in to shed some light on the powerful stories I hear.

Rachael walked in for her second session, skinny jeans tucked into her ankle boots and streaks of lavender in her hair. She leaned back this time, comfortably placing the navy pillow in her lap to stroke like a cat. She looked up at me with a strong confidence and told me the best news: "I threw away my razors."

Her razors. The ones she had been using for years to chip away at the pain inside. Her eyes held a glimmer of hope for the first time in a long time. The smile on her weary face was genuine, one that didn't fade fast and that brought tears to my optimistic eyes. See, Rachael had come to me a month before saying she felt unworthy of people's time, love, and care. She was questioning how long she could continue living this way, and that scared her, so she found help. She couldn't articulate where this feeling originated, but it was ruling her life.

For months she had been coping with the lies by making scars all over her body for a quick escape, but she craved more than this cycle that left her marked with haunting memories. So one day after unleashing it all in her journal, she gave it up. Something holy happened in her heart that day, and she explained the release she felt after our previous session, when she had shared her story and allowed herself to feel again. She found hope amid her struggle, and the razors lost their grip on her life.

The pain roused Rachael from her enslavement, and suddenly she wanted more from life.

> ≫ **How is your pain waking you up? How is your unsettledness pointing to something underlying?**

If we look back to the beginning of the Old Testament book of Exodus, we find hardworking Hebrew people under the rule of a powerful Egyptian king (pharaoh). If we look at the big picture, their day-to-day life didn't differ much from our brutal nine-to-five. The Israelites became slaves in Egypt after Joseph, a descendant of Abraham, died and a new pharaoh rose to power. This pharaoh felt threatened by the Israelites' sheer numbers and feared they might one day attempt to revolt against him. So he placed taskmasters over them to oppress them with forced labor.[3] The Israelites complied because it meant that their daily needs would be met somewhat. Every day they worked was a desperate means for survival. They had buried their dreams long ago (four hundred years to be exact) and were robotically moving along, doing the next thing to get by. Yet they were individual people with souls, created in the image of our Creator. They were a deeply loved people who had lost their identity in the machine of their culture. *Sound familiar?*

We lose sight of who we were created to be when we fail to remember we have a Creator.

As a result, there is a great need for counseling. People are sitting in my office feeling overwhelmed, seeking help, and trying to make sense of all the anxiety they experience. They almost always want me to hand them a self-help book or a formula. They become frantic when I don't provide the step-by-step process to full peace, yet we are too complex for a quick-fix solution.

Instead we practice sitting still. They share the depths of their aching, and I listen. They look up at me with longing, as if to say, *Please help!* I ask them in reply, *What do you want?*

So here we are again, back to that word: *want*. And we are back to trying to *sit still*.

The word *want* means to have a strong desire for something, to suffer from the lack of, or to wish or demand the presence of something.[4] The verse that comes to mind is Psalm 23:1, one of the most quoted Scriptures in the Bible: "The LORD is my shepherd; I shall not want" (ESV). Yet we do want. We want more and more and more.

So again, I find myself asking my clients that inevitable question: *What do you want?*

To answer this question a person must sit in all they feel for more than a passing moment.

What usually follows is a variety of responses listing specific desires unique to the person. However, there is always a common theme of wanting to feel peace and enjoy life again.

We crave wholeness. We want to feel comfortable in our skin. We long for shalom, a gift of peace that surpasses our emotions in the moment.

two

WHERE DOES OUR HOPE come from? In his letter to the Romans, Paul writes, "I consider that our present sufferings are not worth comparing with the glory that will be revealed in us. For the creation waits in eager expectation for the children of God to be revealed" (Rom. 8:18–19).

I clearly remember the first time I read these promising yet lofty verses when I was growing up. I was in a dark room, desperately flipping through the pages of my Bible and hunting for an answer to why I felt so alone. I found myself clinging to the words "glory that will be revealed" but could not fathom what this would be like. Then the words of my Bible's section heading caught my eye: "present suffering and future glory." I instantly spouted off half a dozen examples of my own personal struggles and how I wanted to experience some relief. Not only did I want a breather from all life was throwing my way, but I wanted others around me to catch a break too.

A few days later I was sitting on the floor in my friend's living room and we were doing a study called *Experiencing God*. I had signed up because I really wanted to learn more about this loving God everybody around me was saying is so great. I was confused at this point in my journey, though, because the way I felt and the pain I saw around me didn't match up with a God who was supposed to be about love. I was frustrated and unconvinced. I felt hopeless about the longing in my heart that I could not alleviate. I was overwhelmed for my friends who were dealing with such intense grief within their own stories. I didn't understand why my family pretended like we had it all together when we were struggling just like everybody else.

The verses we read that night also happened to be from Romans 8, and the words were inescapable. Verses 22–25 talk about how we eagerly anticipate what we do not yet have and how we groan inwardly (and at times outwardly) as we await what is to come. I remember feeling so bitter as I considered how a God who loves us so deeply could trap us on this rock. In the in-between space this side of heaven, we live in a world that offers so much and yet so little in its ability to fulfill our deepest cravings. I grew cynical and wondered what the point was in even striving to reach goals and attain dreams in this life if they would always leave us wanting.

That night I left my friend's house confused, with weighty theological questions and a halt in my adolescent spirit.

> » Have there been times in your life when the state of the world or your heart left you hesitant to believe that you would ever feel relief? Take some time to name what comes to mind and release some of that tension on the page.

> » What helps you personally hold on to hope when darkness lingers and the light is hard to find?

>> How have you experienced joy in the wait and anticipation of what is ahead?

The Grander Narrative

It took many years before I began to realize that this wasn't what God intended when he created us. It wasn't some cruel joke. I remembered what I learned as a child—that he had created the garden of Eden overflowing with abundance.[5] God told Adam and Eve they could eat of any tree in the garden except the tree of the knowledge of good and evil.[6] He lovingly gave them a choice, yet they grew greedy. The serpent tempted them in their weakness and convinced them that the Creator was holding out on them.[7] They chose to eat from the tree of the knowledge of good and evil, and we would have too. Evil entered the world, and so did death. As a direct consequence of their choice, we became separated from the God who made us and called us by name. Life itself became painful, and we became slaves to sin because we strayed. So now *we ache.*

Today we tend to look back and blame two people for making a reckless decision that has collectively changed the course for all humanity. Yet we personally repeat the same choice every day in our own corner of the world. We push the limits and we play God. The same evil one lurks and feeds us lies, trapping us in perpetual cycles of pain. Somewhere along the way we've started to believe that our own stories of brokenness define who we are.

Somewhere along the way we've started to believe that our own stories of brokenness define who we are.

Our current story line becomes our default mode. We settle for the lie that we will always be bound by brokenness and that our unhealthy habits are inevitable. The problem then shifts to blaming others, and maybe even God, for our current state, and we completely bypass our own condition of sin that we inherited at birth. We refuse to consider that we might just be settling for a cheaper version of what God had in mind when he designed us as his beloved sons and daughters, and we wallow in this false reality for years—sometimes for a lifetime.

For decades I somehow missed the fact that I was broken, living in darkness in most areas of my life. I grew up as a "good girl." I (for the most part) obeyed my parents, worked hard in my classes, and tried to love the people around me. However, I was blind to my own ego, my judgment of others, and the discontent that was constantly stealing my joy and my ability to live in the beauty of the present moment. I was always living for the next thing and craving the next quick fix to dull the pain I felt deep inside. I scrambled for control whenever something was about to escape my grip.

We each do this every day in our own mind-set and rhythm of life. We tend to believe the lie that the enemy first suggested in the garden: *God must be withholding.*

We are spiritual slaves and yet we all have a story within God's grander story.

Weary

Recently, an old client appeared on my schedule, someone I had not met with in years.

As Lauryn walked in, I was transported back to her very first session just after her dad had passed away. Worry and weariness were written all over her face. Lauryn was pregnant, and what should have been happy news was turning into one of the most anxious seasons of her life. It was playing out in the form of panic attacks, paranoia, and rage. So here she sat with her feet up on the chair across from my couch, sipping water, tears flowing.

I asked her, "What do you want?"

She said, "I want my dad to be here."

We sat in silence, our eyes locked. With her hand on her belly, she wrestled with the reality that every milestone in her life moving forward would inevitably sting without her dad there. She was happy about her pregnancy, but she didn't know how to handle all the emotions that had been unleashed in her upon hearing the news. She thought she had let go of the sadness and the anger she had felt toward God. But now it had all come flooding back, and her hormones were not helping either. Her eyes were focused on the pain she felt, and the ache of grief was so overwhelming that she was finding it impossible to be fully present and enjoy the little life growing inside her. She was at a loss for how to stop internalizing all the pain and enjoy her life again. She felt disconnected from her family and from Jesus. But as Larry Crabb writes in his book *Shattered Dreams*, "Solid ground beneath the pain of shattered dreams is the revelation of mystery; it is the realization that it's more difficult for Christ to restrain himself from making all our dreams come true than for us to watch them shatter. At our moment of worst pain, Jesus' pain is worse."[8]

There is something about being authentic and openly sharing where we're at that releases a tiny taste of freedom we didn't even realize we were missing in our souls. Too often we find ourselves feeling an emptiness and anxiety that we cannot seem to shake. It's as if the enemy whispers in our ear that we are failing and too weak to handle our own life. Believing this long enough will send us into depression. Our bodies naturally react and try to release the angst.

Lauryn's biggest struggle was that she had been keeping everything pent up inside. She felt like she should be happy. She tried to keep busy and act like everything was okay, but too much was stirring in her soul to go unnoticed. The panic attacks exposed her feelings. At this point she felt embarrassed that she couldn't hold it all together. She felt out of control.

Why do we wait until we hit rock bottom before we allow others to enter into our mess?

Maybe it's because we believe a lie that says we must keep all the plates spinning or there might be something wrong with us. But when it all falls apart, we are left lonely and isolated, longing for the community we truly needed every step of the way. Even then we hide and don't want people to know we are struggling. We suffer silently and our anxiety increases. We don't want to admit to ourselves that we need help. We convince ourselves that we are messing up other people's plans; ironically, however, when we allow others to help us in our time of greatest need, they are blessed in the process. I have experienced this firsthand. When people around me need help and they allow me to enter their messy places, I get to see God at work in their lives. It can be easier to see God working and providing in other people's lives than in our own.

At these times I remind my clients of the distressing but true words in Romans 8:36, where Paul writes, "For your sake we face death all day long; we are considered as sheep to be slaughtered." It is a tender nod to the war being waged—a war in which the enemy will try using anything to his advantage and break the person in the process. This is the opposite of God's love for us.

Lauryn may not have felt like she literally was facing death all day long, but figuratively she was. She could barely breathe and felt like she couldn't remember life before her dad died. She couldn't remember what joy felt like, and she was lost without it.

Although she was battling hormone-induced anxiety, she also was fighting with the shattered image that she could actually hold everything together in her life. She was enslaved by the lie that she had more power than the God who created heaven and earth. In her disorientation and pain, she had so easily forgotten *whose* she was. She knew these things in her head, but her heart was hesitant to let the truths sink in too far. She was in self-protection mode and didn't even realize it. This put her in a vulnerable state. She rejected most any hope that tried to creep in.

When we find ourselves in a place similar to Lauryn's, our tendency is not to slow down but to become busy, fueled by adrenaline. We set goals and reach them, we work hard and earn money, and we even volunteer at church and school to feel generous. These efforts are not bad in and of themselves; actually, they are all delightful things to do. Yet at some point we shift into relying too heavily on the earthly rewards they bring and lose sight of our greater purpose in life. *We are surviving but not thriving.*

Think back to the Israelites—it didn't take long for them to assume a new identity as slaves once their daily oppression started. They grew accustomed to the expectations placed on them by their Egyptian oppressors. They lost sight of God's promise that one day they would return to the land of Canaan, their true homeland—a land overflowing with milk and honey.[9] They gave in to the mind-set that putting their heads down and working hard was the only logical way they could survive.

From the outside looking in, a great tragedy was taking place. They were a displaced people with disconnected hearts and minds. They were numb and enslaved, but they pressed on. They found comfort in the predictability and familiarity of their daily tasks. The busyness kept them afloat, and even though it was mundane, they stayed alive by operating as robotic shells.

We lose our way and we forget what we already have.

As Lauryn sat there that day, she somberly stared at the antique-white wall in front of her. The wall was tall and thick, like the barrier in her soul that blocked her from experiencing joy. Yet she said she knew there was something deep in her being that wasn't ready to give up the fight. She honestly confessed that while she tried to believe God was nearby, she was far away from wanting anything to do with him.

Somewhere along the way she vowed to just put her head down, take care of her responsibilities, and trudge along as a wounded bystander. She shared her fear that she might feel like this forever and that her only saving grace was to *surrender.* Her dreams had faded and she grew weary. She was waving her white flag.

We lose sight of who we are.

That evening session was a dip into a season of intense oppression and a "dark night of the soul"[10] for Lauryn. Sometimes healing means allowing all the feelings to flood and then sitting with them for a while. The timeline looks different for everyone, but the goal is to not stay frozen here forever.

We forget how to be whole.

Since brokenness first penetrated the earth we inhabit, all creation has been aching. "We know that the whole creation has been groaning as in the pains of childbirth right up to the present time. . . . But if we hope for what we do not yet have, we wait for it patiently" (Rom. 8:22, 25). As we rewind back to Genesis and the garden, we see where God told Adam, "Cursed is the ground because of you; through painful toil you will eat of it all the days of your life. . . . By the sweat of your brow you will eat your food until you return to the ground, since from it you were taken; from dust you are and to dust you will return" (Gen. 3:17–19).

This pain and anxiety took a toll on Lauryn all day long. She was unraveling. She longed to restore herself back to her rightful place—to escape the captivity she felt. She ached to remember the truths she had tucked away—that light overcomes darkness and that God is good, even in the heavy times. She couldn't calm her anxious heart on her own. All the prayer, essential oils, deep breaths, vitamins, and distractions in the world couldn't heal her imbalanced body and soul.

She needed God every moment to get through the day.

Just as Lauryn had something unexpected shift the course of her life story, I'm guessing you've had your own experiences that have caused you to stand back and wonder why.

You may or may not have lost a loved one like Lauryn did, but I bet you have felt anxious about something out of your control. You may not cope by hiding your pain from those close to you, but maybe you lash out in anger or overindulge in your work to numb the ache. The Israelites in Egypt didn't have our modern-day conveniences to help them dull the pain as they endured backbreaking labor and longed to be restored, but I assume they had their own ways of desperate self-medicating.

The truth is that Rachael, Lauryn, the Israelites, you and I—we all have something in common: *we are human.* We are all broken people living in a broken world that shocks and harms. We all find ourselves hoping for something far better while trying to remember who we are and what we were made to do. We crave relief and hope. We cry out with the psalmist:

> I lift up my eyes to the mountains—
>   where does my help come from?
> My help comes from the LORD,
>   the Maker of heaven and earth. (Ps. 121:1–2)

Take a few minutes to *sit still* and digest. Pray and ask God to help you just *be* with him.

re:story

1. Are you longing for more? What does your longing look like?

2. What do you want? Make a list. Dream a little.

3. Are you aching while you wait for what you want? How so?

4. How are you finding relief? Numbing out? Hiding?

re:sound

"The Dark Before the Dawn" by Andrew Peterson

brick
+
mortar

I HAVE HOPE

They made their lives bitter with harsh labor in brick and mortar and with all kinds of work in the fields; in all their harsh labor the Egyptians worked them ruthlessly.

Exodus 1:14

"Let us come alive
to the splendor that
is all around us,
and see the beauty
in ordinary things."

—Thomas Merton

three

AS WE SAW IN CHAPTER 1, Moses was on the run after killing an Egyptian. He fled to the land of Midian, and soon after he sat down to rest at a well, a group of seven sisters surrounded him. They were there to draw buckets of water for their father's sheep, but some shepherds emerged from the field and drove the girls away. Moses came to the sisters' rescue and watered the sheep for them. When the women told their father Reuel what had happened, he invited Moses to eat with his family as a gesture of gratitude, and he later offered his daughter Zipporah to Moses as a wife.

Moses and Zipporah soon had a son and named him Gershom, which means "I have been a resident alien in a foreign land" (Exod. 2:22 CSB). Moses found himself scattered from his original family roots, but now he was setting up camp with a new family. Life started making a little more sense again.

Back in Egypt, the pharaoh died. The Israelites felt the whiplash of all their years of hard work, while barely being nourished and cared for in their labor. God heard their cries and hope began infiltrating their hearts.

Meanwhile, Moses was tending his father-in-law's flock in the wilderness. When he neared Horeb, the mountain of God, Moses hurried his steps to take a closer look at a blazing bush. Amber flames danced but the bush somehow remained. His eyes wide, trying to see whether he was awake or dreaming, Moses leaned in. And that's when God suddenly called out to him from the bush. Moses responded, "Here I am." God told Moses to remove his sandals, for he was standing on holy ground. In awe, Moses covered his face with his hands.

I imagine God tenderly yet fiercely telling Moses that he had taken a long look at the desperation of his people in Egypt. He reminded Moses that he had seen their suffering and had not overlooked them. He shared his plan to free the Israelites from their captivity and lead them to a land overflowing with milk and honey. He then charged Moses with the daunting task of being his point man.

The messy and mundane come at us hard every day. We all have dreams of what we think life will look like when we grow up, but it turns out a little different in most cases. We have responsibilities that require more of us than we can handle, so we put our head down, work hard. We shove away every ounce of pain we carry and try to ignore it. We deny ourselves the time to really examine the motivation for what we do every day. Our dreams fade like a hot air balloon drifting farther and farther from view. Like the writer of Ecclesiastes, we find ourselves asking, "What do people get for all the toil and anxious striving with which they labor under the sun? All their days their work is grief and pain; even at night their minds do not rest. This too is meaningless . . . a chasing after the wind" (Eccles. 2:22–23, 26).

I met Sara when she was about twenty-four years old. She walked into my office with her strawberry blonde hair pulled into a tight side braid. She sat on the edge of my couch, her leather tote hugging her hip and the weight of the world on her shoulders. Sara was an art and design student who spent most of her undergrad days pulling all-nighters, living from project to project. She had a driven, type A personality and claimed to never fail at much. You can imagine how vulnerable she must have felt to call me in the first place. I asked Sara one of the first questions I always pose to a new client: *If I gave you a magic wand to wave over any part of your life today, what would it be, and why?*

Sara said everything in her life seemed to be going according to plan. She proudly shared how diligent she was, and how her focus helped her scale the design ladder of success. However, she was sitting on my couch with an unsettledness she couldn't shake.

Sara's identity was wrapped up in the work she accomplished daily.

I don't know about you, but when my job or my way in the world becomes a measure of my worth, I start to feel burdened by the endless pressure that requires. It's easy for me to crack under all the striving, especially when my efforts fail or I compare myself to others.

We can easily slip into this mind-set because of the cultural vibe around us. From kindergarten on we are told to work hard to earn the life we want. It's part of the beauty of living in a country where we have choices and freedom to get education and craft the career we feel drawn to. But as with any good thing in life, balance is necessary. Once we start heading down the slippery slope of believing that our role in life defines us, we can start to live as if our happiness is up to us. We crave rewards and pats on the back for our efforts.

Sara said that she was having a hard time sleeping, and when she sat at her desk in the art studio, her hands had begun to tremble. She knew this was not her norm, and *her inability to control her body was a signpost* to a deeper problem. She needed steady hands to do her designs smoothly. She went to see every doctor she could think of for relief, yet all her symptoms remained. So a friend who had been in therapy at my practice referred her to me. She explained that she was not here to talk about her feelings; she just wanted to get to the bottom of her sleep and hand issues. She looked at me with eager eyes and an urgency that demanded help—fast!

I felt for Sara in this moment. We all want the thorn removed so that we can move on with life and do the work we feel called to do, right? We all want the quick fix and the easy answer.

Give me a formula. Give me the reasons why. Give me everything you've got right now to make it all better, so we can all just move on with our lives and stop being stuck here!

But what happens when our circumstances don't change? When there isn't an easy way out?

Numbing out our pain comes in so many ways; we don't even realize we are doing it. Numbness slowly invades our life and we become addicts to the quick fix. This is one of the craftiest ways the enemy attempts to break us down. He doesn't want us to find hope.

We can get so lost when we forget who we are and who we were made to be. We don't even realize how the enemy subtly lures us into his ways of false living, and we settle for a cheapened version of life. We start living in a way that does not reflect our true nature. We lose our sense of self and start acting on impulse, never considering the impact of our decisions. We may be someone who naturally encourages other people, but then we end up living for ourselves and forget about how we can love those around us. Life becomes more about our own survival and less about impacting the world and being a light to others.

At this point in the Exodus story we see a harsh oppressor who ruled over hundreds of thousands of Israelite slaves, forcing them to make mud bricks in the dry desert day in and day out. Alec Motyer defines oppression as "to bring them low" or "to beat down."[1] Clearly, the Israelites were barely surviving and in distress from the intense, mindless workload. Exodus 2:23–25 tells us:

> The Israelites groaned because of their difficult labor; and they cried out; and their cry for help because of their difficult labor ascended to God. And God heard their groaning; and God remembered his covenant with Abraham, with Isaac, and with Jacob; and God saw the Israelites; and God knew. (CSB)

God *saw* his people. He knew what they carried.

This is a moment to pause and name the provision that is taking place in Egypt. God's willingness to enter in and hear the hearts of his people is a form of *manna*. He is God and he does not owe us that gift of his presence, yet he offers it constantly. We tend to only see the circumstances, and we miss the love he shows us by being *with* us in our suffering. Even during the daily grind, he is near. He does not abandon us. Even when we try to separate ourselves from him, he remains.

Although the Israelites were exhausted from the daily trauma and stress of forced labor, life was predictable. Every morning when they woke up they knew what the day held. They didn't have to wonder what to do; they simply had no choice. When a person is living in physical captivity, they also quickly become enslaved emotionally and spiritually. We saw this in Sara's story, as she was defined by the work of her hands. When her hands were unable to perform, she unraveled. I wonder what would be different for Sara, for the Israelites, and for us if we cried out with the psalmist:

> Yes, my soul, find rest in God;
>   my hope comes from him.
> Truly he is my rock and my salvation;
>   he is my fortress, I will not be shaken.
> My salvation and my honor depend on God;
>   he is my mighty rock, my refuge.
> Trust in him at all times, you people;
>   pour out your hearts to him,
>   for God is our refuge. (Ps. 62:5–8)

Yet this was not the mind-set of the Israelites as they toiled in Egypt. They were unable to see clearly and were blinded by the harsh circumstances of their captivity.

>> **What does your crying out look like when your circumstances shift and you start to unravel?**

>> **How is God speaking to you in the midst of your suffering? How is he getting your attention?**

Paralysis

Maybe today you find yourself crying out, swept up in your own daily grind. You might be trying to sort through how you got into this mess in the first place. Perhaps some parts of your life feel smooth and joy-filled, but at the end of the day you find yourself heavyhearted, wanting more, wishing things were different—or even better, craving peace and joy.

>> What do you tend to do with all the thoughts swirling around inside your mind every day?

>> Are you someone who internalizes and doesn't share with others how you are actually feeling? Or are you someone who externalizes and floods those around you with every thought?

>> Do you proudly carry the weight of your worry on your shoulders like a badge of honor? Or do you release the burden and reveal parts of your heart to your closest friends?

We all respond differently to our work and responsibilities. We all have various expectations we put on ourselves and goals we want to reach. The work itself is not bad. The way we view it and the pressure we put on ourselves to handle it all on our own is what breeds unhealth and anxiety.

We see this all the time with those who live in the spotlight. We watch actors, politicians, and musicians make mistakes as a result of their work-related stress. We roll our eyes when *The Today Show* covers yet another celebrity couple's divorce. We shake our head when the front page of the *New York Times* reports that another movie star has died of a drug overdose.

But are we really all that different? *We all have our stuff.*
Some of us pretend to be better than others, and some of us creatively disguise how we really feel. But I can guarantee if we were to sit together at a coffee shop for at least thirty minutes, it wouldn't take long for our stories to unfold and the truth would be uncovered.

I spent the first twenty-plus years of my life trying to pretend that everything was okay. I had it down to a science, and my core belief was that I needed to always have a smile on my face. It didn't matter if I had spent the whole night crying, no one would know because I kept on going.

The work itself is not bad. The way we view it and the pressure we put on ourselves to handle it all on our own is what breeds unhealth and anxiety.

I thought that being a good Christian meant that I needed to constantly appear happy. After all, why would anyone want to be a follower of Jesus if it meant life would still be hard?

In my twenties I fully bought into a consumer Christianity. I literally believed that if I made good choices, then good things would surely come my way. I was one of those people who expected life to operate like math: A + B = C. In this false reality I felt like I had all the control. I was a girl on a mission, out to save the world with a tiring religion of moral efforts. All my success and happiness was dependent on how hard I worked at my life. I found out quickly that this mind-set can only carry you for so long. This lifestyle leaves the soul in want.

I was in high school when I shed my first tear in front of one of my dearest friends, who I had known my whole life. Stephanie and I had matching sunflower shorts in fifth grade and played on the playground together every single day growing up. She was my go-to person, yet I still always held back. Fast-forward to my junior year of high school, when she was dropping me off in my driveway after a student council meeting one afternoon. She asked me if I was okay, because I wasn't acting like myself and probably wasn't smiling as brightly as I usually did. I remember debating whether or not I should tell her what was on my mind. I don't know what came over me in that moment, but I got brave and told her that the night before I had received the hard news that my aunt Diane, who had a spinal cord tumor, had come out of surgery—paralyzed.

I was heartbroken over the fact that life didn't work the way I thought it should. I wondered what that meant for me moving forward, since my morality didn't always equal positive and predictable results. My aunt's new way of living in the world rocked me in ways I didn't realize at the time. Everyone has their way of responding to tragic events in this life, and mine was intense.

I was mad.

Why would God allow this to happen? Why did my aunt have a tumor in the first place? Why, after traveling all the way to New York City to have it removed by one of the best doctors, did she come out of anesthesia unable to walk? My views of God started to shift, and I questioned him a lot.

The smile that was always one of my daily accessories I now left at home some days. I was on edge and lashed out at my family without reason, not even knowing where the anger stemmed from.

I cried, hard.

Yes, *I* cried. I cried in front of my friend Stephanie. For the first time I was *not alone* when I cried but in the presence of another person, who could have reacted harshly or not known how to respond.

But what I found in that moment was raw, real comfort that I had not previously experienced. It was unfamiliar and scary, yet it felt good. Stephanie, who had dark brown eyes and a calming spirit, leaned over and just hugged me. She didn't try to say the right thing or make the situation appear better than it was. I thanked her for the ride and walked into my house with a shift in my spirit that night.

I now felt free to reveal my heart to others in a new way. I felt more connected to friends who had shared their struggles with me along the way.

I was warming up to the idea that God was still present, even in the hard and heavy.

Life felt a little fuller. It was unfamiliar, but I was warming up to the idea that God was still present, even in the hard and heavy. Although it was painful to face the facts, it was *real.*

Stephanie created a space for me to share my heart by simply asking if I was okay. By taking time to really see me and let me feel, she was a form of manna to me. To me she was the hands and feet of God, who promises that he is "close to the brokenhearted and saves those who are crushed in spirit" (Ps. 34:18). *Not only did she listen but she held the space for me.*

I remember getting daily updates while Diane was still at the rehab center. We were all hopeful she would make a full recovery, and some days good news fueled that belief. But one day I was told that she was finally coming back home to

North Carolina. She had a new treatment plan that included an electric wheelchair and house renovations that would enable her to live life paralyzed from the waist down.

My aunt came home a changed woman. Yes, she was in pain, suffering and grieving the loss of her ability to walk. But she had a *new outlook on life*. She was grateful for the smallest glimmers of hope and the gift of life every day. She has taught me over the years to be thankful for good books and magazines, the thrill of hunting for shells on the beach, and the goodness of our God—even when life as we know it comes to a screeching halt. She lives life *fully* and has found a new lens through which to view the brokenness and beauty around her.

She has shown me what it looks like to find manna in our story, even on the heavy days.

My aunt Diane has been a form of manna in my life—a gift of goodness during the chaos and a constant reminder that when life turns out different from what we expected, there is hope!

>> How might you be feeling paralyzed in your life today?

>> What are the circumstances that you can't seem to change? Is it something related to a relationship you can't seem to fix? A diagnosis you have received? A friend who won't forgive you?

>> Whatever the situation is, can you see how it might be stealing life from you today?

>> Do you long for more? Do you believe you were made for more?

What if you don't have to feel this way forever? What if there is hope right here, right now?

Those are big questions that can stir up a lot of emotions. Breathe deeply as you journal your answers. Sometimes, like with Diane, sitting in the struggle awakens us to newfound hope.

four

WHEN I WAS IN COLLEGE I felt overwhelmed by circumstances I could not control but that seemed to be controlling me. I felt like raging waters were rising, and I needed a safe, unbiased person to help me safely process everything going on in my life. Someone who could hear my whole story without inserting their own agenda.

Soon after I opened the Pandora's box of my emotions, I realized there were a number of things that had happened in my life that deeply impacted me but that I had suppressed. Until then I hadn't realized how trauma of any level influences our lives. I started looking back over my life's landscape that was strewn with loss of all shapes and sizes.

When I was in middle school, dear friends from church lost their mom to cancer. Early in high school my sister lost her friend in a car accident. Toward the end of high school, just after the news of my aunt's paralysis, a friend died after an arson fire in her college apartment. I attended the memorial service and wept.

At the time when all these tragedies were happening, I wasn't self-aware enough to know that they were shaping my worldview and deeply impacting my view of God.

The grief all caught up with me in college. That's when I realized I was battling an underlying sadness that I had never attended to. It was time to share my heart in a real way and uncover the pain.

Finding a Safe Place to Process

I entered a season in which I willingly chose to delve beneath the surface and dig deeply, *slowly*. Dan Allender says, "Tragedy always moves our story forward in a way that shalom [peace] could never accomplish."[2]

I grew tired of pretending that I was always happy and that life with Jesus was smooth sailing. I had been convincing myself of this lie for way too long and I wanted some relief—fast.

Through Spirit-led therapy I was able to come to terms with my broken heart. Yes, it made me feel raw and vulnerable, but it revealed parts of myself that I didn't even know existed. Much of my grief had deep roots that could not be uncovered all at once. At times it felt fruitless, but what I gained through revisiting hidden parts of my story has been invaluably healing.

This resurrecting of deep wounds and patterns in my life was gut-wrenching, but my counselor served as a form of consistent manna as she took my hand and we looked back into the dark *together*. She allowed me the time and space I needed to process slowly and find the light.

Ben, my boyfriend at the time (and now my husband of nearly fifteen years), saw it all. Although he would rather avoid pain at all costs, Ben rose to the occasion. He had a way of *listening to me and letting me cry* that was a gift to my soul back then. He continues to be manna for me today, as his type-seven Enneagram complements my type-four tendency to get lost in all the heaviness.

This is the beauty of us being made differently yet both in the image of our God. If we were made the exact same way and shared the same lens in life, we would not be able to support each other in this essential way toward transformation. The Enneagram has shown us how to appreciate each other and value our differences. Suzanne Stabile writes, "All relationships—those that truly matter and even those that don't—require translation. And if our interest in relational growth and transformation is sincere, then the Enneagram is one of the most helpful tools available."[3]

If we were made the exact same way and shared the same lens in life, we would not be able to support each other in this essential way toward transformation.

As we have matured, *the Enneagram has served as a bridge* to bring us back together when we couldn't understand each other's lens in life. It has given us language to name the unique ways we each live life, which has broken our hearts for each other in the best way possible. God knew what he was doing when he matched us together in his master plan.

» Who do you trust in your life? Who are your people you can share your whole self with? Take a moment right now to make a short list of people in your life whom you could invite into this process with you.

We were not made to do this life alone. As the writer of the book of Hebrews says, "And let us consider how to stir up one another to love . . . encouraging one another, and all the more as you see the Day drawing near" (Heb. 10:24–25 ESV).

We need our people.

God is with us along the way[4], but one of his good gifts is the help of friends. Be prayerful and intentional about who you might ask to join you. Be confident that they will feel honored to enter into your story and will be blessed by it.

Our heart and soul are *sacred*. They are not meant to be poured out to just anyone. Today on social media we find ourselves in a reality crisis of sorts. We have access to so many stories that at times it can be daunting and debilitating. The noise can get so loud that we can forget who we are as we compare our story to everyone else's. Social media can also be a gift, because it provides us with a window into people's hearts, even from a distance. What if today you stepped out first to go against the tide in your circle of influence? You could intentionally reveal something about your life that has been hidden from your friends or family. Or maybe you simply pause to look closer into *your own community around you* and start to uncover what is really underneath the surface.

By choosing to intentionally look for God's provision in your story, you are also making the choice to "look up and look around," as my pastor Michael Flake always says. It would be easy to become a navel gazer, just putting your head down and focusing only on your own stuff. And while there can be a season for that, you can't do it forever without a cost. It's restorative when we begin to share our story, and it results in freedom for others to share their stories too. When we *look up and look around,* we can see the common thread of our humanity.

≫ When do you find yourself getting stuck in your own story? How might you look up and around?

Day In + Day Out

I think the fact that you picked up this book means you are looking for support. Like the Israelites, you've grown weary of making bricks day in and day out. And if you were to look to your left and right at the people around you who are slogging through their day to day, you would see that they also need a friend to share in their story. We can choose to carry the weight of the world on our own shoulders, but eventually it will ruin us. If we can learn to bear one another's burdens in community, our load will be lightened drastically.

When I *heard the Lord whisper* to me years ago about writing this book, I started thinking about you and your people. The ones right in your town who you meet for coffee and cry and laugh with. I know we might not know each other personally, but I do know that we are all human and share similar core desires, and because of that we are connected. I spent so many years robotically living the life I thought I had to live. Yet so much more fullness was available to me once I took time to look deeper and harder into my story. And beyond my story and your story is God's *greater narrative* that undergirds our daily efforts as we long for home and for something beyond what we see on the surface.

We are all part of God's story, which makes us interconnected.

There is abundance to be held in our hearts and hands that I want you to find as together we hunt for manna.

Many of the Israelites were enslaved not only by the power of Pharaoh but also by the daily trauma of their forced labor. Since they were human, just like you and me, I can assume that they asked many of the same questions that we do every single day. They longed for *escape*. They ached for something *more*. And yet they were ironically comfortable too.

They settled for less subconciously because they became blinded to the reality that they could experience more. Over many years in an enemy land, they lost their sense of identity and could not see what was happening. By outward appearances they were functioning well as a unified group who all looked the same and complied to the unspoken ways of the world, yet they had no idea there was a richness they could tap by leaning into God and choosing to take hold of a different way of life, even doing the daily grind.

But here is the good news: we weren't all made to do the same thing day in and day out. God made us uniquely in his image, and he doesn't desire for us to mindlessly lift heavy bricks and break our backs all day long. Jesus didn't come so that we might continue carrying burdens. He came that we might have life to the full *and that we might find rest in him*.[5] He did not create us to labor in vain but to work according to his high call.[6]

>> How are you settling in your life? How are you laboring in vain?

>> Where in your home life and/or work life have you become blinded to the truth that you were made for more?

We make our own form of bricks, day in and day out. We don't see how we are a mass of broken people under the mesmerizing control of an invisible enemy who is in a battle for our heart before our feet even hit the ground each morning. We don't see how restless we feel in our bed at night. How sitting numbly at our desk during the day, or even mindlessly running from place to place, is another form of cultural captivity that is subtly yet powerfully overtaking our people as time marches on.

My greatest hope is that together we will learn to *wake up and shift our lens* so that our vision will come into focus and we will truly live. Life should not be a burden we have to bear until we get to heaven. It should be as joyous as driving on a country road with the windows down, the music blaring, and the wind whipping our hair! We can experience joy even while, or especially while, we work every day. When we step into our calling, joy follows.

Sometimes waking up requires us to zoom out of our own story to see God's bigger story. If we can step back and consider that our own circumstances are not so unique after all, that our individual stories are woven together and connect us to one another, we can find more freedom. But first we have to see. We must uncover the patterns and find what's paralyzing us.

It's all manna—God providing *his vision* so we can see again and realize our true identity.

Digging deep to reveal story lines that have been hidden for years isn't like drinking a warm cup of tea. No, it usually feels more like ripping off a Band-Aid. You may prefer the quick rip to get right down to the wound. Others may prefer the slow tug that hurts less but prolongs the process. Either way is better than not taking off the bandage at all. It takes *courage* to look and see what is causing your pain.

We are all in different boats when it comes to understanding our story. If you don't feel ready, you have full permission to close this book for a while until you are. Delve as deep as you like. I pray that you will hear the Holy Spirit speaking louder than anything you might read online or in a book. The Spirit speaks to us through the words of Scripture, if only we will listen and discard any distractions that might come our way in the process.

So why not dive in now, if the Spirit nudges you? Instead of prolonging the inevitable, face the truth before life feels even more chaotic. I see this journey as a preventative vitamin that will help you now and in the future by deeply revitalizing every part of your being before the false narrative grips you tighter.

Start by asking the Lord if this is what he would have for you right now in this season of your life. Find a few people you trust (friend, spouse, counselor, pastor) to walk through it with you. Prepare your heart and mind for what will unfold— both the expected and the unexpected—and hold on tight for what will rise to the surface. This is where full life is found, in the risk of stepping into the unknown to *be* known. As Julia Cameron has said, "Leap—and the net will appear."[7]

re:story

1. What does the daily grind look like for you? Where do you see hope?

2. If you could wave a magic wand in your life, what would you change?

3. Where do you see manna and glimpses of glory in your mundane?

4. Are you ready to delve deeper into your story and uncover what's hiding beneath the surface? If so, pull out the list of people you might want to join you on this journey and ask them.

re:sound

"Your Labor Is Not in Vain" by The Porter's Gate

mighty hand

I AM SEEN

But I know that the king of Egypt will not let you go unless a mighty hand compels him. So I will stretch out my hand and strike the Egyptians with all the wonders that I will perform among them. After that, he will let you go.

Exodus 3:19–20

"Earth's crammed with heaven,
And every common bush
afire with God;
But only he who sees
takes off his shoes."

—Elizabeth Barrett Browning

five

AT THE BURNING BUSH God proceeded to lay out the detailed plan he had for Moses to lead the Israelites out of Egypt—from plundering the wealth of their Egyptian neighbors to providing for every need that might arise on their journey home.

In that moment Moses panicked. He fumbled around trying to convince God, the great *I Am*, that he was not the man for the job—that he was not equipped or capable of such a mighty task. An escape plan from Egypt? Maybe God had the wrong guy. Maybe God had overlooked who he was.

But God said for Moses to throw his shepherd staff onto the ground, and it instantly slithered like a snake. When God said to pick it up, it straightened back out into a staff. Then God told Moses to put his hand inside his shirt. Moses obeyed, and when he withdrew his hand, it was leprous. When he repeated the action, his hand became clean and healthy again. These were evidences of God's power that he wanted Moses to show the Egyptians.

Still Moses persisted with excuses: *But I am not someone who speaks eloquently enough.* God responded with blunt truth—that he is the one who makes human mouths and would provide the words for Moses.

At this point Moses begged for God to send someone else. God grew angry, as it seemed no amount of his promised provision was enough for Moses. Yet in love God showed Moses that he saw his need and provided Moses's brother Aaron to be his mouthpiece. So the plan was put in place and Moses would perform the miracles.

His soul now surrendered, Moses set off on the journey back to Egypt with his family in tow. Aaron joined them along the way, and Moses shared with him God's plan to free their people. They gathered the elders of the Israelites, who worshiped God with humble hearts when they heard that God saw them.

A couple years ago we moved onto a *small property* that we had been dreaming about for ten years. One of my favorite parts of our new home are the backyard chickens we inherited. One morning I peeked into the coop and found the nesting boxes empty. As someone who has become accustomed to not buying eggs from the grocery store, I was baffled by this sudden lack of supply. In my dew-covered gray boots, I peered around the corner and noticed feathers all over the wood shavings. The hens were frantically huddled together, and as I approached I realized they were out of food. I was the supplier of their feed and I had failed!

After seeing their desperation that day, I vowed to always provide what they need moving forward. Soon they began to flourish again. The feathers stopped falling and I found eggs in the nesting boxes where they belonged. My love for those chickens grew in their time of need and in seeing them restored. That morning I was reminded of how God heard the groans and cries of his captive people, and a few things have stuck with me.

First, the hens came together in a group and waved me down as a mass of moving feathers. If they had spread out individually around the coop and tried to manage their hungry bellies on their own, I might have stumbled on a less lively bunch that morning. But by gathering together, they survived. They needed each other to make it.

We need each other when we find ourselves stuck in a cycle. We were made for relationships.

When I think about the Israelites and the daily labor expected of them, I imagine the people would have given up if there were not others around them who were also just trying to survive. Their work was robotic, mindless, and physically intense. They probably hated having to build temples for the pharaoh, a leader they didn't respect. Yet they *endured*. They knew that the daily grind would provide for their basic needs. At this point in our Exodus journey we will see how God's deep love for his people came in the form of demonstrating his power.

We need each other when we find ourselves stuck in a cycle. We were made for relationships.

Second, those chickens depended on me daily, knowing that I was the supplier of all they needed. When they looked around and couldn't find food, they became stressed out and disoriented. They started struggling physically because of their lack of nutrients.

Obviously, humans are much more complex creatures than chickens, but we also need provision and care to grow. We need our Maker to meet us in our need and sustain us beyond our strength.

We all have emotional, spiritual, and practical needs that require us to tap into resources beyond our own strength. We reach ruts in our life where continuing as usual doesn't pan out. We need the power and help of Someone who can break down the invisible barriers that keep us bound in captivity.

Moses is a prime example of someone who could easily fall into living out of a victim mind-set, believing that the world and maybe even God was out to get him. Because of the pharaoh's oppressive regime, he was under a death sentence before he was even born. But Moses carried on the legacy of his family, who were hoping in an option other than death. They fought for more and knew that God was calling them to trust him first.

God uses our stories of deliverance and freedom to point to his mighty power.

It isn't always easy to surrender our plans, but it's incredible to see what unfolds when we have faith. God uses our stories of deliverance and freedom to point to his mighty power.

Powerless + Unseen

Bella had called me a few years before she and her husband Scott finally ended up in my office. She initially reached out because she said they were having a hard time getting pregnant and were getting to the point of giving up. For the first few years of marriage they had been content being just the two of them. They loved their jobs and their life together, and the thought of adding in children seemed daunting and stressful.

Until one day when waves of nausea and exhaustion all pointed to pregnancy and Bella and Scott were thrilled with the news. Unfortunately, by the time of Bella's first prenatal appointment the doctor couldn't find a heartbeat. They had lost the baby they already loved.

Everything slipped away in an instant. Devastated and heartbroken, they each handled their emotions differently. They agreed not to tell anyone, because pretending like it didn't happen made it hurt less—at first.

Fast-forward to the day Bella and Scott walked into my office in marital crisis.

Scott reported feeling like he didn't know Bella anymore and that his only option was to bail. Bella found herself in a desperate place of insomnia and anxiety as a result. She didn't know how to make herself feel better in order to be present for Scott. Clearly they were giving in to the illusion that self-protection would indeed protect them.

They both admitted that they had walked away from their faith and grown bitter. Coming to counseling was their last-ditch effort to try to get their lives back on track. They seemed to be asking: *Why would a God who loves us allow all our friends to have families yet cause us to experience loss upon loss?*

Ann Voskamp describes such desperation in her book *The Broken Way*: "Forget God, and you can lose your mind and your peace. Forget God, and all you remember is anxiety. Anxiety can give you God-Alzheimer's. Forget the face of God, and you forget your own name is Beloved."[1] Bella and Scott came looking for a rescue—for someone to remind them who they were and to again find meaning and purpose in their lives after a season when they felt overlooked by God.

I asked them both a simple yet complex question: *What is your goal for our time together?*

Scott, wearing a disheveled plaid button-up shirt, looked stone-faced out the window. Slow tears streamed down Bella's cheeks as she reached for the tissues on the marble table to her left.

We sat in this space for what seemed like forever. No one said a word. We just sat still in *silence*.

Unspoken sacred connection was happening in all our hearts. Tears welled up in Scott's eyes after a quick glance in Bella's direction. In that moment they found each other again, and there really wasn't much else to say other than letting it be. God provided just what this grieving couple needed that day. A space to be together. *A space to cry.* A space to slowly start to heal. It was an honor to give them permission to stay present in the moment and not rush on to the next thing or fill the room with empty words. We all felt the gift of manna in tears.

Worthy

In Exodus 3–4, Moses found himself in the presence of God at the burning bush, and God spoke directly to him.

His reaction? *He hid his face.*

Sound familiar?

It's as if we are back in the garden with Adam and Eve, who hid because they could not bear to be in God's presence after the fall.

Where might you be hiding? We all do it, of course; it just looks different for each of us.

» Are there times when you feel like the mess of
your life is just too much for God to see? How do
you cope with the shame and guilt that try to take
root in your life at these times?

I think it feels easier for me to walk around faking it most
days, when in reality I am just hiding. Hiding from friends
and family, hiding from myself, and trying to hide from God.
Sometimes we can feel like we are "both too much and never
enough" as Jess Connolly and Hayley Morgan say in their
book *Wild and Free*.[2] When we live out half-truths and walk in
a false identity that is not our own, we are hiding from other
people. We fear that if they see who we *really* are and what
we *really* think, they won't like what they see. What if they are
disappointed? What if they find the ugly hidden underneath
our facade?

We need God's compassion and unrelenting love to provide
us with *courage* to show up and be seen.

I imagine Moses felt a similar fear when he stood before
God in the blazing flames. He recognized that the powerful
Being burning in front of him knew his whole story. Moses
could hide his face, but he could not hide his backstory. God
knew everything that Moses had done in Egypt. God knew
every detail about his life and yet was still calling him to lead
the Israelites. Moses felt unqualified and guilty. He didn't think
he was the person to do this job. He offered every excuse
imaginable. He lacked confidence and focused on his flaws
to try and avoid God's calling.

I don't know about you, but there are many days when I
wake up and don't feel *worthy*. I ask myself all the time, *Who
put me in charge of everything I am supposed to steward well?*

Does God really remember all the ways I've messed up and how my heart turns ugly on a dime and how I so easily forget to trust him and all he has done in my life? I relate to Moses and how he pleaded with God to find someone else to lead the masses.[3] We each have our corner of the world, territory that God has entrusted to us for his glory. For many of you that may be loving the people in your office or in your neighborhood. For others it may be the people beside you in class or the kids you pick up from preschool. None of us feel qualified 100 percent of the time, and we find ourselves making excuses.

So what do we do with that paradox, knowing we can have an impact but also knowing we are weak?

As we look back at Moses and hear him fumbling over his words, reminding God about his stutter and pulling his brother Aaron into the equation, do you see your yourself in his struggle?

Maybe someone else can just do this for me.

Maybe I can just keep my head down and clock in and out and try not to ruffle any feathers.

Maybe I can just do the bare minimum to get by.

But what happens when God calls you higher and deeper out of his great love for you?

>> How might God be doing this in your current season of life?

God *saw* Moses. He knew the ugliness in Moses's story, yet he still called Moses to follow him.

Moses needed God's mighty power to enable him for the task at hand. We do too.

This *calling* is a form of manna; it's an opportunity to find a richer life instead of settling for less. It was by God's holiness and power that Moses was able to go back to the people and share with them the promises of their Creator. God provided just what he needed to do it and more. Moses had no certainties, but he had faith, and that's what kept him going.

What kept Moses humble was remembering who made him, who called him, and who provided manna along every step of the journey. In the same way God equipped Moses, he gives us all we need through his mighty power and his ability to see farther down the road ahead than we can.

God saw Moses. He knew the ugliness in Moses's story, yet he still called Moses to follow him.

Six

WHEN MOSES AND HIS FAMILY arrived back in Egypt, he and Aaron approached the new pharaoh and delivered God's message to let the people of Israel go back to their homeland. Pharaoh refused exactly as God said he would and made the Israelites' labor even harder as a result.

The next time Moses and Aaron approached Pharaoh, they performed a miracle that began a series of events we call the ten plagues. Aaron threw down his staff before Pharaoh and it became a snake. When Pharaoh's magicians did the same thing, Aaron's snake-staff swallowed all the others.[4] This was like the starting pistol at the beginning of a track meet, and it sparked a battle of strength between those who held power among the people.

Pharaoh was determined to keep the Israelites under his control in Egypt. The first five plagues included the Nile turning to blood, swarms of frogs, gnats, and flies, and the death of all livestock. After each plague Moses gave Pharaoh the opportunity to change his mind, but God hardened Pharaoh's heart. The next five plagues were boils, hail, locusts, darkness, and the death of all firstborn sons.[5] That tenth plague hit too close to home for Pharaoh, and his heart shifted once he realized how relentless God was to set his people free.

Before the final plague occurred, God gave Moses instructions for the whole community of Israel. Each family was to take the blood of an unblemished lamb and smear it across their doorposts as a distinguishing mark on their household.[6] This occasion is called Passover, because when the tenth plague struck, every Israelite family who had done as God commanded was *passed over*. Every Egyptian household—including Pharaoh's—lost their firstborn son, and there was great anguish and wailing in all of the land.[7]

This marked the official start of the exodus, for in the middle of the night Pharaoh summoned Moses and Aaron and told them to take all the Israelites and their livestock and leave Egypt to go worship their God. He even told them to take everything of value from the Egyptians on their way out. Six hundred thousand Israelites fled Egypt that night with their *hands full*. They set off into the desert, eager to praise the God who saved them.[8]

If this is not a foreshadowing of the greatest love story ever told, I don't know what is. In the New Testament, when John the Baptist saw Jesus walking toward him, he declared, "Look, the Lamb of God, who takes away the sin of the world!" (John 1:29).

Sometimes standing in the shoes of those who have gone before us tethers us to our ancient roots and gives us fresh eyes to see that our stories are not so different from theirs. The stories of Scripture remind us that what we battle is our *humanity*, not just our own personal suffering or circumstances.

This is one of our first glimpses of a New Testament reality foreshadowed in the Old Testament. We get to see that Jesus is the true Passover Lamb whose blood covers us from all forms of judgment by paying the penalty we deserve. In their book *Echoes of Exodus*, Alastair Roberts and Andrew Wilson explain, "The Passover is an obvious prelude to the work of Christ. It is about redemption from slavery by the blood of the lamb. . . . Israelite families were not saved by their personal godliness that night or even by the amount of confidence they had in God. They were saved simply by the fact that the blood was over their house."[9]

God's people had become comfortable in their captivity and were blinded to their true identity while living under Egyptian oppression. And now God had spared their lives by the blood of a lamb just before leading them out of slavery. It was not by their moral code or how many times they gave to the poor. It was not about their abilities. It was about *God's power*. His mighty hand.

It was all manna.

Looking back, we can clearly see God's unmerited mercy in the form of the Passover that leads to the exodus. We can see what the Israelites could not yet see: God was with them and offered them forms of manna uniquely suited to their need. Their hands were *full*, yet their disorientation left them confused and complaining.

God had started the long, loving journey of wooing his people back to him, yet they felt aimless. Their eyes, which had been focused upward on God's power, now shifted back down to their hands. They looked not at what they had but at what they were missing. They suddenly were flooded with the effects of their traumatic years of oppression and did not know who they were without their daily routine.

We see such disillusionment in our own culture as we base so much of who we are on what we do to earn a living. But when a person welcomes God into their story, *they start to see their greater purpose and gain a vision* for how to move ahead. The Israelites reluctantly left the comforts of what they knew, even though it hadn't been comfortable at all. It had been grueling. But it was what they had come to know as their security, and it was their *identity*. They only felt known by what they did, not by *whose* they were.

They didn't know that if they took God's hand and followed his path, they would get to experience life on a whole new level, with wonder and awe as their everyday companions.

Where We Fix Our Eyes

Many of us let what we do each day define our story. It's the first question we ask when meeting someone for the first time: *What do you do? What's your job?* As if the only way we can distinguish ourselves in this world is to claim identity in our profession. Yet this is a brutal lie.

We are more than the work we produce or the vague versions of ourselves that we portray. We were made by a God who holds the world in his hands. A God who numbers the hairs on your head, the grains of sand on the shore, and the stars in the sky. And he holds us.

One piece of wisdom we can learn from the Israelites dipping their toes into a fresh taste of freedom is that before we can find true peace, we have to remember *who we are.* Ann Voskamp writes, "Beloved, you are the

Before we can find true peace, we have to remember who we are.

re-membering people. Find your feet. Find His face—His broken-wide-open heart of communion."[10]

So instead of shifting our eyes back down to what we lack, what if we tried to fix our eyes on Jesus and remember who we are, beings made in his image. This connection with our Creator helps us find our grounding, especially when we lose our sense of self or we experience trauma. We need God. We need the truth that he will always be who he says he is, that he will remain the same in our ever-changing circumstances. He longs to be with his people, and part of being in any healthy relationship is trust. Taking time to read his Word and relish this reality seeps deep into our bones and helps us plant firm roots of truth that we can endlessly tap into.

Promises of God's love are evident throughout every intentional word that is displayed for our constant consumption. The abundance and interconnectedness of each story we read is manna. The men and women in the Bible who have wrestled with losing and finding their identity in Jesus are visual examples of the redemption that we can find at our fingertips. At any moment of any day, we can take hold of *God's love and goodness* that flow from his power.

What a gift!

If you are looking for ways to fix your eyes on Jesus, take some time right now to do these grounding/connecting practices:

1. Sit still and pay attention to your breath rising and falling in your whole being.
2. Thank God for what you have physically within yourself and tangibly around you.
3. Open God's Word to find the promises you need to remember.

4. Listen to the song at the end of this chapter and take some time to journal.

5. Take a few more minutes to let God's words water your soul until you swell with joy.

May we remember who and whose we are as we continue to embark on the Exodus road together. May we allow the power of our mighty God to break down the barriers in our being that keep us from his best for our lives. May our stories start to shift as we learn to trust his mighty hand.

re:story

1. Write about a time in your life when you've seen God's power in a mighty way.

2. How did you relate to Bella and/or Scott in the way they each dealt with their pain?

3. What feels like a plague in your life right now, an interruption worth paying attention to? What is it revealing to you about yourself and about God?

4. What do you make of the Israelites being blind to all the manna they held in their hands upon heading into the wilderness? When do you do this in your life? List some ways.

5. If you are honest, where have you lost your sense of self along your journey so far? Where/how have you seen hope cracking through?

re:sound

"It Is Well" by Kristene DiMarco and Bethel Music

tribe by tribe

I AM FREE

That very day God brought the Israelites out of the land
of Egypt, tribe by tribe.

Exodus 12:51 Message

"We don't have to do it all alone.
We were never meant to."

—Brené Brown

Seven

THE ISRAELITES HAD ESCAPED the control of Pharaoh and now fled into the desert *tribe by tribe*. Not one by one in isolation, but together, side by side, communally, men, women, and children.

The Bible says six hundred thousand soldiers and their families traveled together on foot and had not prepared any provisions for themselves. But God once again provided for them in specific ways that only he could anticipate: "Then he brought Israel out with silver and gold, and no one among his tribes stumbled" (Ps. 105:37 CSB).

Exodus says that the Egyptians pressured the Hebrews to go quickly and gave them whatever items they asked for, hoping to escape death themselves. The Egyptians were questioning the power of their own gods after witnessing the power of Israel's God.

At this point the Israelites had been under the oppressive control of the enemy for over four hundred years.[1] Generations of God's people had known only captivity. For mothers and fathers, grandparents and great-grandparents, slavery was their way of life, and they had nothing with which to compare it. They were used to getting up every single morning, grabbing breakfast, and heading out for the manual labor they had to do, whether it was crafting buildings or cleaning a king's chambers. Freedom was something they had never known, so this was unfamiliar territory.

> » Can you imagine how disoriented the Israelites might have felt being free after all those years of slavery? What does it look like for you when you enter new territory in your life?

Finding Freedom Together . . . Tribe by Tribe

It may be impossible for us to grasp literally, because most of us have never made bricks without straw or built temples for kings. But I would argue that we can all relate. What about that nine-to-five job where you methodically punch in and out each day? Or the classes you attend?

Do you ever feel like something else has control of your every move and thought? Do you find yourself waking up at night and feeling stressed, already panicking about the next day? Sometimes we just numb out and try to forget what we are feeling to keep going.

When a predator wants to gain power and control over its prey, one of the craftiest ways of doing so is to make the prey *numb*. Under the pharaoh's rule, the Israelites didn't have a clear sense of purpose; they simply did what they had to do to get their basic needs met. They were numb. But once all the people tasted freedom, they started to *wake up*. As the paralysis faded, they came alive to themselves and started to remember who they were again. I envision a group of people waking up in the morning and stumbling out of their tents all at once—*stunned.*

The Israelites probably felt a wide variety of emotions as they entered unfamiliar territory with only a vague sense of where they were headed. I imagine there was a collective vibe in the community of wanting to sprint out of Egypt but also having the option of dipping their toes back in if they wanted to. I can feel their disorientation in my gut.

Once all the people tasted freedom, they started to wake up.

Think about when new seasons come in your own life. You may have been waiting a long time for things to change, but when change happens it can be scary and uncertain.

When my kids were tiny, every day felt so monotonous. That season was the most isolating time of my life to date, simply because someone else needed me 24/7, and at the end of each day I was *spent.* Being a highly sensitive person,[2] I found the learning curve of motherhood to be especially taxing; all the extra stimulation wore me out and left me lonely.

I remember waking up before the sun one morning, in tears and wanting to crawl back into bed before 7:00 a.m. I'd hardly slept all night, so I already had sleep deprivation working against me. But this was just the beginning of a subtle shift into a dark season for our family, that at first I was not willing to admit.

We are all deeply afraid to let our mess be exposed.

>> **What keeps you isolated? Why do you think you try to do life on your own at times when you need people the most?**

>> Do you tend to hide or withdraw when life feels
overwhelming? How does this impact your friend-
ships, marriage, and family? What do you need to
recharge after a long day of work?

Recently, as I sat working at a local restaurant with my
earbuds in, the booth along the peeling brick wall in front of
me suddenly filled up with toddlers. They were the loudest
children I have ever experienced in my life. Their moms were
at a separate booth, and it was as if there was an invisible
sound barrier between them and their kids. I didn't know
whether to laugh or cry as the clock was ticking until my
carpool duties. However, after observing the chaotic scene
a little longer, the nostalgia won me over. I flashed back to
those days when, for the sake of my sanity, I would throw
on some sweats, pull my hair into a top knot, grab the diaper bag, and go meet a friend with my whiny toddler and
newborn.

The moms in the restaurant that day chose to gather. Even
though it was hard to get out the door, they kept each other
company in the messy mundane of parenting young kids.
While servers delivered sandwiches and salads, these women
laughed about how they had forgotten to brush their teeth or
cried over the sleepless nights they'd had. The kids were happy
because they were sitting with other little people, eating fresh
food, zooming straw wrappers, and living life to the full. They
were all better together versus isolated at home. They needed
eye-to-eye, smile-to-smile, touch-to-touch connection. It was
beautiful—and loud—to watch.

It was quieter when they left, but I instantly missed the
contagious joy they had shared with me.

Life can be full of chaos, yet it brings a fullness that we might not otherwise have known. Joy and sorrow and everything between those two extremes make up the fabric of life and bind us together.

Sometimes other people become our earthly lifeline to hope and act as the hands and feet of Jesus to us. Gathering together to share our stories helps us remember what is true and can bend our hearts toward worship.

Joy and sorrow and everything between those two extremes make up the fabric of life and bind us together.

May we be people who stay connected even when it's hard. May we let our hidden hurt be seen, share in one another's joys and sorrows, and love loud. May we help those we love uncover the glory and goodness of life.

I startled awake. Next to me, my husband Ben was coughing on musty air, and a few seconds later I heard each of our kids coughing down the hallway. It was the first night in our latest rental house, which had been built in the early 1900s in the tiny town we affectionately called home. With our growing family and my grad school loans, finding a place to live on Ben's full-time ministry salary was proving to be tricky. We were exhausted from wrangling three kids five and under. We desperately wanted to stay in the same school district and raise them in this town where we thought we'd be living for the long haul, when suddenly our plans unraveled.

I started living in an entitled headspace that left me feeling like the past few years of struggle should have somehow earned me the life I wanted. Of course, in retrospect it was just plain ugly and embarrassing. I was scrambling, pretend-ing that I had life under control, when in reality this was my rock bottom.

I was a mess.

When your hormones are raging and you're caring for tiny children, you can't step back and assess what is actually going on in your heart and soul. At least I couldn't. Every time people asked how I was doing, I just told them I felt *heavy*. It was the only word I could find to describe what was weighing me down every single day. Yes, we had some crazy circumstances swirling around in our life. But the hardest part for us all was the internal battle silently being waged in my mind *day and night*.

That morning when I woke up to everyone coughing, it felt like I had bricks on my chest. Ben had refinished the hard-wood floors that were hidden underneath layers of carpet after decades of sketchy renovations, so all our boxes were stacked floor to ceiling in the extra bedroom off the kitchen. The linoleum in the dining room had been ripped out, but we had not replaced it yet because we ran out of time before we had to be out of our other house. Our kids were all sharing one bedroom, but even amid the chaos we were hopeful we could eventually get everything in order and be okay in this rental until something better came along. We tried to convince ourselves it had great potential.

Unfortunately, as the coughing intensified I realized that we must be dealing with a mold and moisture problem. I knew it had to be invasive if we were all reacting so violently after just one night in the house. My motherly instincts went into full force, and I told the kids to get dressed while I roused Ben from a deep sleep. He was exhausted from all the renovations and moving, but tearfully we both realized we were not going to be able to raise our family here after all.

We needed a new place to live, and fast.

So without a tangible plan, we loaded up the car, the kids, and Salem, our pet Weimaraner, and headed to our hometown for the next month of summer. As we were pulling out of the driveway, I looked in the rearview mirror and knew it would be the first and last time we slept in that rental house.

All the stress of the past year flooded me with grief I could not explain. Tears were unleashed from the depths of my being, and all the adrenaline that had given me the stamina I needed to get through this move evaporated. The kids and I headed to my parents' house for the week to *recoup* while Ben headed to Colorado to camp with Young Life. Our life in general was full of joy—raising babies, doing ministry, loving our community that felt like family—but I was struggling to see the light. I knew the problem ran deeper than all of this.

The waves of life can pound us over and over until we feel like toddlers wading into the ocean alone. In my smallness, I felt like the vast water might seize me. Eventually we found our footing and attempted to wipe away the salty grit from our eyes, but we were left with the stinging sensation that takes time to fade. We needed a warm towel to wrap up in and soothe our soul.

In these moments of despair, when the waves are washing over me and the salt is stinging my eyes, I sense *God's presence* the most. I feel alone at first, but then it happens—the peace that doesn't make any sense floods over my body and God provides. There is the manna again.

How does he get it so right, down to every detail? He knows just what I need more than I do.

That day as we hopped on I-40 and headed to my hometown, a special treat of smoothies in hand to offer some relief for our grumbling stomachs and souls, out of nowhere my oldest son started singing—just singing—and my tears began to fall. He has an ability to remember lyrics and every single note that is sung, and that day his gift of music was a gift to me all the way home.

The song "Home" by Phillip Phillips was popular at the time, and my son started out humming that familiar tune. He then ended up singing *a song I had never heard before* but that I am convinced God wrote specifically for me in that holy moment in the car. I fully believe this was God singing straight to my heart through my son. It has happened more than once, and I stand in awe every single time. God knows music is the window to my heart. He knew it would calm me at my core and he provided me with that manna for the moment.

When We Still Feel Alone

When we had to move out of the moldy rental, I felt like I was living in free fall, as if I had jumped out of a plane with a faulty parachute. For someone who likes to have an idea of what's next, I was distraught in the suspense of not knowing. Some days I wondered if the parachute would ever deploy. I felt like I was holding my breath, waiting on something I wasn't sure would ever come to fruition. It was in *this free fall* that I found more freedom. I know it doesn't really make sense, but in my releasing of control, Jesus comforted me. He whispered his words of truth in my ears and provided manna in the form of friends, Bible verses, music, books, and especially my husband, who had a steady confidence in our future. Jesus met me right where I was, moment by moment. *Learning to wake up to his love shifted my perspective.*

I started paying attention to these manna moments and was stunned by what I'd been missing.

That month I shed more tears than maybe my whole life-time put together. Many days I felt like this was going to be our new normal and that I might not ever feel settled again. I know it sounds dramatic—and believe me, that's what I told myself every time I started to feel sorry for myself or for our family. I tried to pick myself up emotionally and convince myself that I should be happier and at peace. It felt like I should be able to handle all this change and uncertainty better than I was, but I just couldn't. My emotions and hormones took over and I had to humbly wave the white flag. The enemy's whispers of self-doubt and shame started to take root in my heart.

In my releasing of control, Jesus comforted me.

Why now, God? Why did we have to move when life already felt like too much to handle?

I just needed a consistent place to lay my head down, to find some solace and rest.

Now it felt like that comfort was all being ripped away, and I didn't have a solution. I could sense that we were entering a new season and that surely God had something better in mind for us than I could ever dream up, but I still wanted to hold the reins. I wanted to have the plan in plain view. A friend had just passed away, work was intense, and I was at the end of my rope. Keep in mind, I had no idea that the property I mentioned back in chapter 5 would eventually become our new home.

At the time it felt disorienting to not know what was next. Fear of the unknown made me tremble.

> » What is up in the air for you today? What feels un-settled and like you are in a free fall?
>
> » What does trembling look like for you?
>
> » Have you had a time in your life when you craved something new but were hesitant to step out of a place that felt more comfortable to you? Do you regret choosing to stay back out of fear? What does it look and feel like when you leap into the dark unknown?

The Israelites found themselves in a similar struggle when they entered the desert. Even with their friends and families walking alongside them, I imagine some days it felt like too much to bear. Fear prevented them from walking confidently ahead, and they began to doubt God's promises.

Persistent Patterns

Sometimes it seems easier to just keep moving forward with life as we know it. We can keep doing life on our own, and it feels like there isn't really a reason to change.

I wish that I could provide a real-life counselor to walk along with you through this book, like a package deal. This is just a reminder that I highly recommend finding someone to invite into this messy journey of looking back, looking at your current life, and looking ahead. Getting support from others will keep you from getting stuck in your own head for too long. In my opinion, every human who walks around on this earth battles anxiety and/or depression at some point in life. It's hard to avoid.

We all want to be told that we are not crazy and that life will make sense one day. But even more than that, we don't want to feel *alone* in life.

The last thing we think we need—but the thing we need most—is for someone to hear our story and stay. Why? Because it means the curtain has been pulled back far enough to reveal that we are flawed, and there is no turning back from that truth. Being seen forces us to realize that we must rely on something or Someone greater to get through. It puts our life into perspective and forces us to come to terms with this reality.

Without realizing it, we each operate under patterns every day. These patterns are mindless habits and routines that seem normal to us. They sweep us up in their enticing web.

We have bedtime routines and a whole other set of patterns in our early and late hours of the day—the things we mindlessly do when we doze off and wake up. From the moment we hear the alarm we will have thoughts that flood our minds as the demands of the day invade. We will all take a deep breath and our feet will hit the ground, but it will look different for each of us. Our perspective will be completely influenced by our outlook on life and the way we operate in the world. We will make a million decisions that are influenced through that lens. It's all about how we see life. What we view and value as the highest priorities have power to determine every move we make.

So ask yourself, What is it that I believe? How is it shaping the thoughts and scripts that are running through my mind when I wake and sleep? How do I determine my next right thing?

Once we become aware of the patterns that persist in our own life, it's as if blinders have been removed. We can start to see why we act the way we do. Our eyes see more clearly, and we have the choice of being transformed by God's grace through the renewing of our mind.[3]

Yet most of us thoughtlessly move through life without much intention, unable to search our soul for the reasons why we do life the way we do. It isn't because we aren't capable of this analysis; we simply lack awareness that more is going on beneath the surface of our actions. Many of us live our life above the surface—I did for years.

Once we become aware of the patterns that persist in our own life, it's as if blinders have been removed.

It is really freeing if you think about it. We are human beings who can uncover parts of who we are in light of the One who made us. Our personality is a deep well. We are complex creatures with many layers. We were all made creatively and have a God who wants to know us and be with us. He longs for us to come to him to find out who we really are and what we were made for. He designed us with a plan in mind; we are not an accident. God has a plan for us.

≫ **What does God have in mind for you?**

≫ **What makes you come alive? What makes you cry? Where do you feel at home?**

These questions point us to *happier and more whole living* as we discover the answers for ourselves. Frederick

Buechner says it best: "The place God calls you to is the place where your deep gladness and the world's deep hunger coincide."[4]

Do you want to keep dreading your alarm? Or do you want to feel expectant every day when it buzzes?

The reality that *God wants to partner with us* in this life is a gift. It is manna. Do you ever pause to wonder how God will amaze you and what he will accomplish through you? I know I do.

When I was in college, I spent the first few years exploring different career options, trying to decide what I would major in. Only after I found myself in a counselor's office and was given a new, life-changing perspective did I realize that working in the mental health field was my calling. I wanted to help others in the way I was helped. The passion this ignited in my soul has been something that only grows with time.

Sometimes we have to view things from the other side of the experience table in order to see the vital need for our calling. Maybe that means making time to intentionally put yourself in the shoes of those who need help.

> » List a few of your passions that come to mind. Ask
> God what your next move might be.

eight

Naming Our Need

There is power in *naming our patterns* and realizing that we are being controlled by a false narrative—a story that we might not actually want to live, that we long to break free from in hopes of living life more fully, wholly, and joyfully. Back in college I did Beth Moore's study *Breaking Free*, where she talks about God being in the business of breaking people free from the chains of generational sin and cycles that weigh us down. She shows us that redemption is a journey that we walk through with Jesus over time. It is not something we can just repair ourselves overnight. It is a process that takes time to uncover and grow in and find true transformation.

Naming what we need is not weakness; it is a colossal step in the direction of wholeness.

As I dealt with anxiety when my kids were babies, I found that I had actually been battling it most of my life. I felt overwhelmed by self-induced shame and didn't understand how to be kind to myself in the struggle. I didn't have to fear the anxiety that so easily entangles; rather, I could acknowledge it and gain perspective. I didn't realize it at the time, but there is a worthwhile way to stop fighting anxiety so hard every day. One of my counseling colleagues, Kurt Zuiderveen, often says that once we become a student or a friend of our anxiety, we are then able to relax and learn from it and see what purpose it serves. I've found that once we own and name our vices, we can unearth the role that they play in pointing us to our Redeemer and refining us. Would I choose to have anxiety instead of just living a peaceful life without worry? Absolutely not. But it's how I deal with my anxiety that enables me to move forward and not be trapped by its torments. I have the choice whether or not to get the physical and psychological support I need. We can learn slowly over time how best to grow as we glean wisdom from what could otherwise paralyze us. There is power in giving yourself permission to be curious about what your anxiety is revealing.

Naming what we need is not weakness; it is a colossal step in the direction of wholeness.

I want to invite you to consider the parts of yourself that you wish were different.

>> **When you look in the metaphorical mirror, what do you see that you wish you could change?**

It is healthy to desire growth in specific areas of your life, but it is essential to notice what toxic scripts play out in your mind that might get loud and drag you down over time.

>> **Do you often find yourself shaking that pointer finger of shame in your own direction?**

>> What do you tell yourself, and with what tone,
when you fall into unhealthy patterns in your life?

What might it like look like for you to take a kinder approach with yourself today? How would it feel to allow the thorn of anxiety to take up space and linger for a while versus using all your energy to try pulling it out?

What does it look like to stare at that thorn—whatever thing that makes us tick and hinders our hearts—and tell it that it does not hold all the power, but that it can play a role in our lives for a season? We can be curious what part it is playing in our life and even ask what gift it might be giving.

The language we use with ourselves matters—each word becomes part of the script that shapes our narrative.

The language we use with ourselves matters—each word becomes part of the script that shapes our narrative.

As we sat together at my dining room table one day, my friend Molly asked me if I could allow my own anxiety to hang out for a little while. Holding my third baby and living in a rental house that would soon not be ours, I was being overtaken by the stress and anxiety of the unknown. Molly gave me the greatest gift: freedom and confidence that Jesus is who he says he is, and that no weapon formed against me shall prosper.[5] She reminded me of what was real and true. She wasn't afraid of my honesty about anxiety's grip on me. She took the time to listen, and *her presence* in being with me brought me peace.

This was a moment when my friend was able to use her gifts with gladness to meet my need. Emily Freeman writes, "Art is what happens when you dare to be who you really are. You have the power to influence, to move, to become. . . . When we live free, we are able to give freedom. When we live loved, we are able to give love. When we are secure, we are able to offer security. God reveals himself through every artist."[6] Molly was manna for me that day when I was at a loss for what to do.

The truth is, anxiety was bullying me with its wit and craft. It had me believing it was in control and that I had lost any personal autonomy over my own mind and body. This intangible emotion, which doesn't have any real power, was determining every move I made back then. I was letting it control me, like a puppet being moved by its strings. But by letting down my guard and allowing Molly to speak truth over me, anxiety lost its grip and I tasted *freedom*. Yes, anxiety still hangs around, rearing its ugly head often, but the power it held over me faded. I stopped giving it control and have now found *full life* even in its presence.

Our Thorns Play Roles We Don't Realize

Lately I've been thinking a lot about the way God uses even the darkest parts of our stories to bring us closer to him. I don't think he wants us to experience life painfully. I do however believe wholeheartedly that he wants to use every thorn for his glory.

The truth is, if it weren't for my hormones and our life circumstances over the past decade, I probably would not have had the gumption to write this book. When people ask me what inspired the idea, my answer is the same every time: because I want others to find hope sooner than I did that will shed light and bring life.

I want you to know that even in your darkest moments, God is with you. He sees you. He knows you. He calls you by name and knows the number of hairs on your head. He knows you from before you were born all the way to the last breath you'll take and the ellipsis points in between. He holds your life in his hands. You have no cause to fear that but every cause to praise him for it.

Once we know our patterns and name our thorns, we can start to unearth the gifts they might bring and find true *free-dom*. The truth is, on this side of heaven we will never know the reasons behind everything that happens to us. We can, however, catch glimpses of the glory and see the hand of our loving God as we unearth the manna in every moment of life.

If anxiety, depression, and hormones didn't exist, we could more easily try to hold it all together. I think about my life up until a decade ago, and I was doing a pretty good job at pretending. I knew deep down at my core that it was only a matter of time before the steam would start revealing itself from the volcano that was my heart. But once my inward and outward life became too much to carry on my own, I couldn't hide anymore. The cat was out of the bag. My true self was emerging. I would never have it all together, and in that truth I found relief.

How humbling yet freeing. It has changed my life to come to terms with this reality.

> » What relief does it bring to your soul when you hear that we can't ever hold it all together?

> » To what extreme lengths do you go to maintain your image and appearance? List them. Be specific.

We don't want our thorns to show. We would much rather tuck them all away, even if they painfully try to poke through like spines on a cactus.

All our pretending deeply impacts our well-being and contributes to high blood pressure and heart disease. We can't internalize our feelings forever; anxiety inevitably surfaces. If we were able to sit together and look each other in the eye, I wonder what you might share with me. If we trusted each other and had the time and space to really open our hearts, I bet we would each have years' worth of words to unload—both light and heavy, joy and sorrow.

Something we are missing in our culture today is real connection. Not FaceTime but actual face-to-face time. There is something about being in a room with another person, breathing the same air and experiencing each other's presence, that creates holy ground. When I am given the gift of sharing a meal with a friend without any agenda or timeline, I get to really see them and they get to really see me. I might not share every detail of my life with them, but I find it very hard to omit the big stuff when someone asks with a kind, intentional heart.

We are so busy with our own to-do list and with work and family life that we have completely lost the art of communicating, even with those closest to us. We have our laptops, phones, and earbuds closing off our senses, and it affects our awareness. People are rarely fully present in a room, and when they are it feels uncomfortable.

There is something about being in a room with another person, breathing the same air and experiencing each other's presence, that creates holy ground.

I recently took a few months away from social media to quiet the noise. In general I am someone who highly values the creative content and relationships I can enjoy online. However, I've found that when I can't hear my own voice or handle sitting still without compulsively reaching for my phone, it is time to take a breather. The first thing I noticed this time was how dependent I had become on mindlessly scrolling while out in public places. I've noticed that when we see someone else holding their phone it acts as a trigger, and we fumble around in our bag or pocket so we can join their unspoken game of subconscious isolation. This is the direct opposite of freedom.

So when anxiety rises and the hormones rage, or when depression weighs us down, we can start to sit back and ask, What can I see differently in my life because this is present? The thorns give voice to what would otherwise remain silent, and because of that I can boldly claim that even our thorns are forms of manna in our lives. God uses it all.

I usually have a hard time waking up on my own to what is really going on in my life. I need my friends and my husband to speak into the more hidden parts of my soul. This requires both vulnerability and a safe place to share my heart. For years I prayed for friends to whom I could bare my soul without fearing shame or guilt responses. It took some time, but I am so grateful for my dear friends who are willing to ask how I am really doing.

If you are longing for the freedom that the Israelites found as they were entering new territory tribe by tribe, will you consider letting down your guard and connecting with a friend (or group of friends) to share your heart with in the next week? Will you look for ways you can gather around a table to talk? Will you attempt to take steps closer and deeper into relationships that bring life?

We need each other so we can uncover all that keeps us from living a life of freedom in Jesus.

1. Who in your life is walking alongside you in a way that you can share about the current state of your heart? If you don't have such a person, where could you find one? Sometimes it just takes asking someone to meet up for coffee and really chat.

2. What lies underneath the symptoms you feel from this ache in your heart? What purpose do you think those symptoms might be serving? How can you wake up to what's hiding under the mask of tension?

3. What does it feel like when you taste newfound freedom? Exciting? Scary? Both?

4. When have you uncovered something about your soul and found the gift of provision in that discovery? Make a list and reflect on each.

5. What are some ways you can practice connecting when you find yourself isolating and pretending?

re:sound

"No Longer Slaves" by Jonathan David
and Melissa Helser

fire + cloud

I AM GUIDED

By day the LORD went ahead of them in a pillar of cloud to guide them on their way and by night in a pillar of fire to give them light, so that they could travel by day or by night.

Exodus 13:21–22

"Truly we live with mysteries
too marvelous to be understood."

—Mary Oliver

nine

As the Israelites left Egypt, God guided them in a different direction than they expected. A straight shot through Philistine country would have made the most sense, but God led them out into the desert. "For God said, 'If they face war, they might change their minds and return to Egypt.' So God led the people around by the desert road toward the Red Sea" (Exod. 13:17–18). It would be like finally getting to leave after work on a Friday to head off on a much-anticipated vacation, then being suddenly rerouted. Imagine thinking you were headed across the Atlantic to Europe and then hearing the flight attendant say you are taking the Pacific route instead. Logically that makes no sense.

After witnessing everything that had just happened back in Egypt and seeing the power God demonstrated by sending the plagues and shifting Pharaoh's heart, I would have expected God to take his people directly to Canaan. He is God, after all, and has the ability and power to protect. He could have arranged some ancient form of a red-eye flight—quick and easy and no one gets hurt along the way—especially after the

Israelites had trusted him. The human mind always assumes
God will meet our expectations *our* way.

There were over a million displaced people wandering in the
wilderness with high hopes of returning to their homeland—
fast. *They had plundered their Egyptian captors, were
told to leave with Pharaoh's blessing, and had hope
for better days ahead.* It was by God's hand that they experienced freedom in the first place, not by their own strength.
Yet the Israelites already had their eyes fixed on the horizon of
what they didn't have. They so easily forgot the fact that they
were free.

Ben and I were heading south from Montana, crossing the
wide expanse of Idaho on US Route 89, also known as America's most scenic road trip.[1] I was looking out the window at
the mountains still hours in the distance when it hit me that
this long detour, though unplanned, was providing just what
my heart needed. We would not have taken this route without
Ben's *ability to make any new path seem better than
our original plan.*

We had flown west a few days earlier from North Carolina,
just after our wedding, with grand plans to hike grassy trails
and ride horses in Glacier National Park. I had googled images of Going-to-the-Sun Road and fantasized about gathering
wildflowers in the beaming sunshine and riding horseback to a
river's edge to fly-fish with my fella. It was the end of May, and
surprisingly we were about to spend half of our honeymoon
blanketed by two and a half feet of snow in Big Sky country
without many groceries or four-wheel drive. To say our first
week of marriage was an adventure is an understatement.

So there we were, riding up and down through the rolling hills of Idaho, the glorious Tetons visible far off in the distance. Idaho was manna for me in that moment—a reminder that the plans we carefully curate are not always what we might need or even most desire. As Wendell Berry writes, "We live the given life, and not the planned."[2]

The plans we carefully curate are not always what we might need or even most desire.

At that point in my early twenties I was still living under the illusion that my favorite out-of-context Bible verse meant I would get *my* way. I naively thought that when God said "for I know the plans I have for you, plans . . . not to harm you, plans to give you hope and a future" (Jer. 29:11), it meant he would give me what I wanted if I obeyed him. Yet no matter how hard I tried, life always ended up looking a little different than I expected.

We knew our honeymoon wouldn't be as smooth as hopping a plane to Turks and Caicos with an all-inclusive package. We were certainly seeking an adventure in the Northwest, but we never expected it would be a snowball of hiccups around every corner. We can laugh about it now, but at the time it felt like nothing was going according to plan, and we were bummed. We had no choice but to drive out into the middle of nowhere and hope for the best around the bend.

That day when we drove through Idaho, we were heading in the complete opposite direction of where we had planned to go, but circumstances beyond our control forced us into a sweet surrender south. I felt out of control in the unknown, which was new to me after living a cautiously measured life up to that point. I could feel my anxiety rising and falling in my chest as we encountered rushing rivers and blind curves.

I may have been kicking and screaming internally, but when the jagged snow-capped Tetons caught my eye, my focus shifted. *I knew deep in my soul that this long journey was leading us somewhere special.* I found myself asking Ben if there was a way to get there faster. Our map said it would be another three hours before we reached Jackson, Wyoming, and I just wanted to be there already. Yet I was starting to learn from that breathtaking ride that *beauty emerged* even before our final destination on the other side of the mountain range, and it was *marvelous.* We may have been exhausted from our travels and the major shift in our plans, but the detour was so worth it.

> » When was a specific time when your plans went
> awry? Who did you blame? How did you react?
> How did things end up shaking out in the end?

I imagine the Israelites might have experienced similar feelings but on a much larger scale. As God's people were learning to trust him and to hunt for the manna in their midst, they remained hesitant. Yet they had seen him provide by the strength of his mighty hand, so they had high hopes that he would not waver in his promises.

A few years ago I sat in an old restored cotton mill and listened to Holly Worsley, a dear friend and one of my favorite Bible teachers, share about Exodus. The fact that she chose to teach on this book of the Bible when I was working on this book was manna in itself. She suggested that God knew an enemy was ahead waiting to attack the Hebrews, and that this may have been why he guided them in the opposite direction. In that moment I realized God has the aerial view. He sees what is around every bend in our life, and he goes before us.

I have found myself sharing this concept with my clients when we get to an honest place in therapy. They say things like, "We have waited patiently for [fill in the blank], and we just don't know why God is holding out on us," or "We have done everything right," or "It's not like I want the whole world handed to me or something." What they are actually saying is "I want what I want and I want it right now." Can you relate? I sure can.

We don't want to wait or wonder. We want our plans to unfold seamlessly, and we think because we dreamed something up, it must be what's best. We think, *I've worked so hard and tried to be so good,* and then we view ourselves as a victim of our circumstances. We want the remote so we can fast-forward to the good parts, because we don't want to relive the past or wallow in the darkness too long.

I also know that simply saying, "Well, God has the aerial view" can sound patronizing at first. If you said that to me, I would mentally roll my eyes. However, if we really sit back and consider that this could be true, trusting that God sees what's ahead of us, we could start to find the peace and rest that we've been hunting for in all the wrong places.

In his commentary on Exodus, Douglas Stuart notes that "God knew [the Israelites'] limited perspectives and naive expectations full well and thus led them away from Philistine territory."[3] This not only affirms that God sees far beyond what we can but also suggests that he can see our *inner* thoughts. Only God has a window into what we really think and believe about him and about ourselves and the life we inhabit, which reveals that what we think matters to God. He knows us well, and in wanting the best for us he lovingly guides us through detours that don't always make sense. Alec Motyer calls him a "companionate God" and reminds us, "It is important to note here that people were not redeemed and then left to their own best devices. The Lord who appointed them for salvation also appointed their onward path, not as a general directive but on a day-to-day, moment-by-moment basis."[4]

Moment by moment.

Yes, God meets us and guides us moment by moment, breath by breath.

So as the Israelites were taking bigger strides deeper into the desert, they began to surrender to the reality that they were going to be *taking a longer route than planned*. This is when the Lord first appears in a tangible way in front of his doubting people. The Bible says, "By day the LORD went ahead of them in a pillar of cloud to guide them on their way and by night in a pillar of fire to give them light, so that they could travel by day or night" (Exod. 13:21–22).

This verse says the Lord *went ahead* of them. He didn't expect them to find their own way in the desert alone. He was with them, *guiding them along every step of their journey.*

At times I have personally felt like I was being led out into the desert, and my past response during such dark seasons was to isolate myself and try to push through it on my own. But when we receive bad news, what if we don't just shake our fists at God but instead *trust* him?

Waiting in the Unknown

Last September the Carolina coast braced for what was forecasted to be an imminent and record-breaking hurricane.

Meteorologists showed everyone maps with red dotted lines tracking the path of Florence. Everything felt like it was moving in slow motion that week, yet life didn't pause. We all knew that we would feel the storm's strength and power in the form of wind and rain—*eventually*. What we didn't know was the exact timing of its arrival or where it would linger. With any massive storm system, spaghetti models of potential paths are all over the place. Our human knowledge can only extend so far and reveal so much ahead of time. The true impact on our communities would be fully known only after Florence wreaked its destruction on the towns, beaches, and roadways of our state.

The disaster was upon us and yet there wasn't much we could do to avoid it.

That Saturday afternoon during the heaviest bands of rain, my heart sank as our large oak trees flung their branches down toward the earth and leaves swirled around our porch. My dear friend Kristin sent me a text message asking if I could chat on the phone. She told me it wasn't urgent, but it was important. She warned me that it was heavy. My mind started to race and I felt like I'd been gut-punched, as if the world I knew was about to make another inevitable shift. Past experience flooded my mind like the rains that were turning my freshly mulched flower beds into a river. I wanted to erase her message. Surely another wave of sadness was not going to come my way and surprise me—again.

So I frantically flipped through Netflix and chose a show for the kids. I asked them to stay on the couch because I had to make an important call. I slowly made my way to the front porch again, praying the Lord would prepare my heart for what I was about to hear from my friend.

I don't remember the exact words she said, but I do know that I felt like the wind had been knocked out of me. I thought maybe I was dreaming—but no, this was a real-life nightmare. She had just been diagnosed with breast cancer.

God, no! No, no, no.

She is healthy. Her family serves in full-time ministry. They have two beautiful kids. No!

There is nothing we can do to avoid these swirling storms. We can try to make a nice tidy life, one that provides all the things we want. We can work hard and earn money to live comfortably. But brokenness abounds. No one is immune to the ripple effect of the fall.

I didn't know what to do in that moment when my friend called me other than to *be* with her.

I knew that she was hurting and that having to tell me and other friends and family was brutal. I also knew that she was disoriented by this heart-wrenching news that was disrupting her life. We were both scared. We didn't know the prognosis, as she would not find out the stage of her cancer until the biopsy results came back a few days later. With the rest of her loved ones, we were forced to continue on daily and hope for the best, with everything looming off in the distance. We had to wait and see what was coming next.

Isn't this the hardest place we find ourselves in life—in the waiting and the ache of the unknown?

It may not be a friend's cancer diagnosis or a slow-moving hurricane coming your way. For you it might be the daily anxiety of not being able to pay your bills or dealing with emotional abuse that you are too scared to walk away from. It could be a looming cloud of doubt that has followed you around since someone hurt you years ago and that makes you question whether you can be successful in life. Maybe you don't yet have words to name what you are battling and carrying, but it is evident that something is not quite right.

Every day we find ourselves in the middle of our story with only a vague sense of what's next.

This may look different for you than it does for me, but I bet there is some overlap. Every day I find myself trying to balance my family, friends, job, and life in general. Add in a desire to create something beautiful that I can share with the world and feeling that I never have sufficient time to do it, and life can be maddening. Choosing to simply drudge through these days can become a recipe for disaster. We become filled with stress, anxiety, and desperation. All we feel invades our soul, and when the longing persists, it points us inward.

Life wasn't supposed to feel this way. It was supposed to be different.

When we walk around living a life less full and vibrant than we expected, we settle for just wanting to get past the pain any way we can.

We might have strongholds that have a tight grip on us and won't seem to let go anytime soon. We become displaced by the ways we operate in life and in our relationships. We want more but we don't know how to get it. We struggle and try every day without relief because we ignore our Guide—God.

What struck me most about my conversation with Kristin that day was that she had a *deep peace* that transferred to me through the phone. It was obvious that she knew God was going before her, a pillar of cloud and fire to light the darkness of this unknown path ahead. She told me the plans for treatment and we hung up the phone.

In the split second I had before my kids' TV show ended, I remember tearfully handing Kristin over to Jesus. I fully believed with her that he has the aerial view and that her health was in his hands.

I believe that there is a sacred and holy reason why you—yes, you—are holding this book in your hands at this very moment. This is not an accident. You were made for more, and the One who made you is bound and determined not to leave you the way you are for the rest of your life. He longs for you to taste the goodness of this life here on earth even in the midst of the heavy and the heartache. He wants to give you the manna you need while you wait to tackle the unknown. Will you let him be your guide?

ten

RECENTLY I SAT with a woman who had sauntered into my office ready to set some goals. Carlee moved my gray plush pillow out of her way forcefully, pulled out her leather-bound journal, and said, "I need your help!" She told me that she was in the middle of making some big decisions about grad school and what her next step would be in life.

She abruptly flung her shiny, straightened hair over one shoulder as she started flipping through her pages of questions to ask me. She obviously had an agenda for our time together and didn't want to leave empty-handed. I felt the tension in the room rise as she expressed her frustration. I could see that she had been running on adrenaline for a long time and that she was utterly exhausted. Desperation was the only reason she was here, and it was a big deal that she was asking for support.

Carlee was the oldest child in her family. She had a type A personality and always achieved her goals. She had followed all the formulas to get into a good college and had graduated a year ago. When I asked her to tell me what adjectives her friends would use to describe her, she responded, "Driven, stressed, and successful." She could own the first two, but what she couldn't claim right then was the idea that she was successful. Just a few months before coming to me, she found out that she was not accepted into the graduate program she had been planning to attend in the fall. The news left her disoriented and confused about the next step for her life.

This wake-up call had spun Carlee into an unfamiliar cycle that she could not seem to break.

Every day she went to work at a job she didn't really love and dreamed about where she wanted to be. She felt out of control at not being able to move forward on the plans she had made. So she just kept showing up every day, beating herself up emotionally because she felt like a failure. She began suffering from a wide range of symptoms, from heartburn to irritable bowel syndrome, and had visited multiple doctors.

Every day Carlee tried to wrap her mind around why she hadn't been accepted into the program she applied for. She was having what looked like a mid-life crisis, but she was only in her twenties. She simply didn't know how to break free from the disappointment she felt with herself. After spending so many years working toward this one goal and then having it yanked away from her, Carlee wanted to give up. But instead she made a list of things she needed to do next to keep going. She rationalized, *If I could get a prestigious internship, then maybe they would reconsider and I could reclaim my plan.*

Unfortunately, even after landing her dream internship in the city, Carlee found herself living in a tiny corner apartment and having panic attacks every time she headed to her job. The woman she worked for was known for her intensity and lack of healthy boundaries, yet she was highly respected in the field of international marketing and branding, and Carlee had placed her high on a pedestal in her work life.

Every morning when Carlee got up to go in to the office, a knot would form in the pit of her stomach. By the time she was making breakfast, she felt like she couldn't eat. As she walked down the creaky stairs toward the subway, her heart would start to race. She complained of feeling dizzy and worried she might pass out before she even got there.

The tears started to fill Carlee's icy blue eyes as she admitted, maybe for the first time, that she was scared and didn't have a plan B. She shared that she was struggling to even make it in to work each day, but she had worked so hard to earn that job. She leaned back against my curvy mauve couch and cried. I was slow to speak because I knew that her *tears* were part of the process of healing and learning to give herself grace. There wasn't really anything that I could say to help her in that moment.

For years Carlee had been trying to hold it all together, and suddenly she couldn't anymore. For the first time in her life she was coming to terms with the unknown.

Carlee knew deep in her bones that there was more for her. She knew that the anxiety she felt wasn't going away anytime soon if she continued in the direction she was headed. Yet she didn't want to give up her dreams or her desires.

Her desires weren't flawed, and I imagine yours aren't either. But like it did for Carlee, I wonder if something might feel off-kilter in your life? Is your body revealing unseen issues? What feels "off" for you?

Is it that you don't know what comes next as you enter a new life season?

Is anxiety or depression crippling you every day?

Do you lash out at your spouse or friend when they don't
seem to understand you?

Is your high-paced job stealing all your energy and leaving you drained?

Do you have a chronic illness or a new diagnosis that you
just can't ignore?

Thomas Merton graciously reminds us that the *darkness
points us to freedom*:

> This is where so many holy people break down. . . . As soon
> as they reach the point where they can no longer see the way
> and guide themselves by their own light, they refuse to go
> any further. . . . It is in the darkness that we find true liberty.
> It is in this abandonment that we are made strong. This is the
> night that empties us.[5]

My heart breaks for my friend Kristin and my client Carlee in
their darkness. However, the thing that distinguishes one from
the other is a relinquishing of control. When Kristin called that
day to tell me she had cancer, she was anchoring into the foundation she has in Jesus. She confidently trusts that he's got her
and that he will be enough for her as she navigates her treatment
and healing. She knows that God will give her manna for every
moment, even on the hardest days. She has let God be her guide.

If you find yourself in a place like Carlee, fumbling around
in the darkness and trying to make sense of your emotions
or your body's reactions to specific circumstances, would you
consider trusting God as a guiding light in your life? I believe
your whole being would calm, no matter your circumstances,
simply because you would find rest in his loving arms.

When Dust Dances

One afternoon I was sitting in what I call our cozy room (inspired by my friend Myquillyn Smith, aka the Nester). This is a tiny room where all my favorite books are arranged by color on built-in bookshelves. I find myself in this room a lot because I always tend to have a book in my hand. I was flipping through one of my favorites when I happened to look up.

Afternoon light was pouring into the room, and I was about to pull the blinds when I noticed that all the dust particles were dancing. It was oddly magical and also disturbing to see all the dust so plainly. I sat back down and just stared up in awe as differently shaped slivers of matter floated in a million different directions in the room. Normally I wouldn't have noticed, but today I was paying attention to the *light.*

I started thinking about manna.

I pondered and asked myself, What if the veil of the invisible was pulled back more often in our lives? What if we could see what is usually unseen? *What if we were able to wake up to the manna in our midst?*

So far we've seen the many ways God provided for the people of Israel, even when it seemingly didn't make sense. We've seen his power time and time again. But we've also seen the brokenness in us and around us.

What if we were able to take our eyes off the horizon, stop focusing so much on where we want to be, and pay attention to where we are? When I slow down and pay attention, I see the manna in my midst more clearly, like the dust dancing in the sunlight in my cozy room.

I'm convinced that God is providing manna in our midst every day throughout our lives, just as he did for Israel. When we are too focused on what's next, we miss what is right here before our eyes. Waking up to the mystery and hunting for manna keeps us awake versus asleep.

Just like when I was missing the natural beauty of Idaho right in front of me because I was so focused on the Tetons in the distance, I can so easily want what's next and miss what is right here, right now.

God is in our midst today. He may not be in the form of cloud or fire, but like the dust in my cozy room, he is dancing. We just don't often have the eyes to see it. I love the image the psalmist paints: "God is in the midst of her; she shall not be moved; God will help her when morning dawns" (Ps. 46:5 ESV). And Zephaniah prophesied, "The LORD your God is in your midst, a mighty one who will save; he will rejoice over you with gladness; he will quiet you by his love; he will exult over you with loud singing" (Zeph. 3:17 ESV).

We can be confident that even when the darkness lingers, we will have a guiding light that will show us the way, and when the sun scorches, a cloud that will block its intensity. Walter Brueggemann says of God's fire and cloud, "Both the day and the night are filled with enormous danger, and this people is completely vulnerable. The cloud shields from the sun; the fire protects from darkness."[6]

God knows what we need more than we do. When we can take an honest look at where we are in life and admit that we cannot do it alone, we will then be living out a richness of freedom that only God can offer us. This requires having faith and trust in an invisible God who makes himself visible every day. "Now faith is confidence in what we hope for and assurance about what we do not see. This is what the ancients were commended for. By faith we understand that the universe was formed at God's command, so that what is seen was not made out of what was visible" (Heb. 11:1–3). If only we would wake up and notice!

Waking up to see the manna God provides is simply a matter of recognizing what we already have. When I start to see it, I stand in awe of the glory and grace of our God and am compelled to worship him in any way I can. Whether by writing, dancing, singing, talking, or just being, let's invite God to be our guide so that we might reflect him with every good gift he has given us.

May we consider the detours and where they might be taking us in our soul journey today.

1. When was a time in your life when you felt like God was taking you on a detour?

2. Where do you find yourself questioning God's goodness in your life right now?

3. Do you see yourself relating more to Carlee or to Kristin in your life right now? Why?

4. What are some examples of manna in your life that you have awakened to lately? How does your discovery of these gifts cause you to worship God? Be specific.

5. Write about what it might look like for you to lean into the mystery a bit more and to trust God to guide you. List some practical ways to do this.

re:sound

"One and Only" by Jess Ray

dry ground

I AM PROTECTED

Then Moses stretched out his hand over the sea, and all that night the LORD drove the sea back with a strong east wind and turned it into dry land. The waters were divided, and the Israelites went through the sea on dry ground, with a wall of water on their right and on their left.

Exodus 14:21–22

"We each need to find our own unique ways of giving expression to the storm inside us."

—Sue Monk Kidd

eleven

WE HAVE COVERED a lot of ground in the Exodus journey so far. We watched God rescue Moses from death on the Nile River. We saw God free his people from the slavery of Egypt by sending plagues and the gift of Passover. We saw God plunder the Egyptians and provide all that the Israelites needed to be equipped for the desert journey. We watched him reroute an entire mass of people to avoid a hidden enemy. Now we find the Hebrew people standing by the Red Sea, wondering how they will get across. Egyptians pursuing them from behind. Either direction they looked seemed bleak.

Suddenly they could not seem to remember God's provision that had gotten them this far. Their eyes were fixed rearward on the army that was advancing against them. It appeared the enemy might prevail after all. I imagine despair, doubt, rage, sadness, and hysteria were taking over.

But as they stood there, God inserted another plot twist. What they would experience in that moment trumped everything else that had happened.

I had just taken our middle son upstairs to tuck him in for bed when I heard the first knocks on our front door. My husband serves on staff with a local ministry called Young Life, so we have relationships with a lot of high school and college students. We had received news earlier that day that a young girl we knew committed suicide. In a matter of minutes there were over a hundred weeping teenagers crammed into our tiny house, packed in shoulder to shoulder.

When I made my way quietly down the stairs after tucking our boys in for the night, all I heard was the *tender voice of my husband Ben* praying and tears softly hitting our hardwood floors.

Sometimes the waves of life crash so hard that our bodies and minds cannot make sense of it.

When I was in college, one of my favorite songs that we would sing with our friends at Young Life was rooted in the words of Isaiah 43:

> Do not fear, for I have redeemed you;
>   I have summoned you by name; you are mine.
> When you pass through the waters,
>   I will be with you;
> and when you pass through the rivers,
>   they will not sweep over you.
> When you walk through the fire,
>   you will not be burned;
>   the flames will not set you ablaze.
> For I am the LORD your God,
>   the Holy One of Israel, your Savior. (Isa. 43:1–3)

Sometimes it feels like the waves are going to consume us, doesn't it? Like they just keep crashing and life becomes more than we can handle. It is in these moments when we are most like the Israelites, thinking our safety and security are up to us. This is an alarming spot to land in life.

Sometimes the waves of life crash so hard that our bodies and minds cannot make sense of it.

People call my office every day and share some version of a restraining fear. They attend a few sessions, open up about their life, and as we slowly start to uncover past pain they begin to experience some release from its grip. When this happens it can be overwhelming, like when the Israelites first stepped foot out of Egypt. The first thing I encourage my clients to do when they enter this new territory is to find a few people who can walk through the desert with them. I can help to guide them through their story when they are in my office, but when they leave and reenter their daily life, they also need a community to hold them up when they can't support themselves.

Things tend to start off smoothly as we begin to make these connections between their past and present. Self-awareness can be healing in itself, as it explains the reasons for some of the feelings we experience that we didn't see before. But soon after this fresh perspective wears off, people tend to become fearful. It feels like trying on new glasses with a new prescription. The headache that results until your eyes adjust is not a good feeling; it's uncomfortable.

We want to get unstuck and stop feeling the way we do, but what is required to get to that place is intense. It's as if all the shadows of our story are pushed into the light, and it can feel quite dark.

Alec Motyer says of the Israelites, "The world around them had more valleys of darkness than it had green pastures."[1] We want life to be full of all the green pastures, and we long to live in the garden of glory again. It's what God wants for us too. He is constantly pursuing our hearts to lead us home. He has put those desires in us and they are not something we need to shake off. But to appreciate the green pastures, sometimes we must first wade through the valley of darkness.

So just as the Israelites found themselves standing at the edge of the Red Sea, we find ourselves standing on the edge of doubt that rises when darkness hovers. We want to believe that God will continue to be faithful and provide what we need, but sometimes our world makes it hard to fully believe that he could provide a way out of the stress and circumstances we battle.

> » Has there been a time in your life when you felt like you were at the end of yourself?

> » What were/are the waves crashing over you? How did you cope and make it through?

Are you facing a big project at work or a difficult situation with a friend or spouse? Do you feel like you are at the end of yourself right now and do you wonder how you'll survive? If that's you, please flip to the back of this book to find some resources I have handpicked for you. Sometimes trying to find help and support is like looking for a needle in a haystack. My desire in writing this book is to help people like you who might be ready to ask for help but are afraid for anyone else to know. I pray that you will listen to that small nudge in your soul that says you are worth receiving care.

All too often we suffer in silence, and that is <u>when we are most at risk of letting the darkness win</u>. We desperately need to "fight back at the lies with truth," as my friend Ellie Holcomb often says. Sometimes we can do that on our own by taking the time to read the promises of God in Scripture and letting his Word wash over us. Other times, however, we need the help of our family and friends and church body to help us wake up to what we might be missing. There are

Listen to that small nudge in your soul that says you are worth receiving care.

also times when the struggles we face require reaching out to a doctor or professional counselor who specializes in helping people in need of more experienced support.

God isn't looking for us to clean up our lives and get ourselves all together before we come to him. How silly would that be? It would be like handing me a stack of fresh white towels and telling me to wipe off all the mud before I get into the shower instead of just stepping into the water to get clean. Life is the same way. God is eagerly awaiting our decision to just let him set us free from everything that is holding us back in life. He longs to make us new.

> » When is a time you felt like you needed to clean up before you could approach God?

> » Is there anything still keeping you from revealing your whole self to him and accepting his love?

When Fear Forces Us into Fight or Flight

The Israelites stood at the edge of the sea and cried out that God had brought them into the desert to die. What forgetful people they were!

It's easy to sit here thousands of years later and say that God was going to be faithful to his people, *because we know how that story panned out.* But what about in our own lives? When we find ourselves flooded with fear, our body is forced to flee or fight. When our whole being senses a threat, our brain triggers a release of adrenaline. This process happens more quickly than we realize, as one Harvard Medical School article explains:

> After the amygdala sends a distress signal, the hypothalamus activates the sympathetic nervous system by sending signals through the autonomic nerves to the adrenal glands. These glands respond by pumping the hormone epinephrine (also known as adrenaline) into the bloodstream. As epinephrine circulates through the body, it brings on a number of physiological changes.[2]

Our bodies were not designed to exist in this hyperdrive mode as much as they do these days. If our system stays in a heightened state for too long it can have harmful effects on our bodies. I can imagine the Israelites' adrenaline was pumping when they realized Pharaoh had a change of heart and had sent his chariot army after them. Their bodies must have flooded with anxiety. Exodus 14 records,

> As Pharaoh approached, the Israelites looked up, and there were the Egyptians, marching after them. They were terrified

and cried out to the LORD. They said to Moses, "Was it because there were no graves in Egypt that you brought us to the desert to die? What have you done to us by bringing us out of Egypt? Didn't we say to you in Egypt, 'Leave us alone; let us serve the Egyptians'? It would have been better for us to serve the Egyptians than to die in the desert!" (Exod. 14:10–12)

The Israelites cried out in fear. Walter Brueggemann has an interesting perspective when he explores this concept of the Israelites *finding their voice* in desperation. He reveals to us another aspect of their crying out:

> The Israelites do the only thing they can do, the thing they always do in fear, and the thing they did before: They cry out to Yahweh. Their cry is characteristic of Israel's faith, modeling the way in which the troubled turn to God. The slaves have now found their insistent voice. They cry out to Yahweh in protest, complaint, demand, and hope.[3]

Every kind of crying out matters to God. He hears his people when we let it all out. Pain at times can be a privilege, as it *awakens the heart to feel and call out* to our compassionate Creator. We all want relief from the pain, yet we also know the Author of all our stories is in control; so our natural default is to call on him in our moments of greatest need.

The Israelites' adrenaline was pumping fast and their nervous systems were in flight mode. Their first route of escape disappeared instantly as they saw the dust from Pharaoh's chariots clouding up over the hills. Their next move was to blame Moses for bringing them to the desert to die. They even went so far as saying that they hadn't wanted to leave Egypt in the first place. They made it sound like they were living a life of luxury as slaves, when in reality they had been in oppressive captivity every day of their lives. At this point in the story, they were not yet fully free. They were still entangled by the illusion that settling for less in Egypt was better than this day of doom and gloom. Any sense of security they had felt fleeting, and they needed protection from their God—*now*.

Doubt's Deep Roots

The problem comes for us when we live in the dark for too long. Deep roots of doubt begin to overtake us, and any manna that we have discovered starts to fade from our minds. The pathways in our brains continue to tell a script that says life is too hard to bear. We start to believe that our story has no hope and we even begin to live out a victim mentality. Life as a victim involves constant doubt. Doubt that you are loved. Doubt that life will ever feel better. And that doubt shifts the blame onto others.

The advent of the functional MRI (fMRI) in the last two decades has allowed neuroscientists to develop a better understanding of brain functioning during certain experiences.[4] We now know from interpersonal neurobiology that when we start to feel something negative, such as a threat to our existence or happiness, negative neural pathways gain traction. The *Journal of Systemic Therapies* explains it like this:

> This bias is believed to be associated with the survival of our human species, whereby experiences of danger can be perceived as more important to retain than "positive" experiences. The tendency to attend to "negative" experiences is thought to

be visible at both the cellular and structural level. The effect of these connections to the limbic system is that an individual can react very quickly to a dangerous situation without thinking.[5]

Essentially, it makes perfect neurological sense that we (and the Israelites) respond the way we do in terrifying situations. This is part of the brokenness from the fall impeding the higher function of our brains in a negative way. Our enemy is crafty in his schemes, even down to our neurons.

twelve

THE ISRAELITES' THINKING was flawed; they thought that by returning to their false sense of security back in Egypt they would somehow find peace. Even making bricks without straw seemed more secure than where they now found themselves—at the edge of a sea with an enemy hard on their heels.

That's when Moses tells them something that initially doesn't make much logical sense: "Do not be afraid. Stand firm and you will see the deliverance the LORD will bring you today. The Egyptians you see today you will never see again. The LORD will fight for you; you need only to be still" (Exod. 14:13–14).

Don't be afraid?

Stand firm?

Be still?

How could Moses remain so steady? Only because he deeply knew and trusted in God, the Maker of the sea, as his protector. The God who numbered the grains of sand on which the Israelites stood and who had safely *brought them up out of Egypt into the wilderness.*

As the Egyptian chariots made their way over the mountain toward the sea, the Israelites stood still, with no other option except to trust that God would fight for them as Moses had promised. God told Moses to stretch out his staff to divide the sea so the Israelites could walk through on dry ground.[6] Here God makes it clear that he is in control and that his plan is for the people to know once and for all that he is God. The Israelites were now waking up to his love and power as they remembered all that had been done so far.

The moved from in front of the Israelites and stood behind them, coming between them and the army of Egypt.[7] What a powerful and loving image of God, choosing to stake his claim for his people by placing a visible expression of himself between his beloved and their enemy! The God of Israel has victory as the waves close over the Egyptian chariots and Pharaoh's forces are wiped out.

As the story concludes, we see the Israelites fearing the Lord with healthy reverence and putting their trust in him and in his servant Moses.[8] When the story opened, Moses had told them not to fear the enemy; in contrast, they now fear the one true God who had come to their rescue yet again. Only in the stillness, when they had a pause after he split the sea, were they able to relax enough to recognize God's presence and power that was providing freedom.

***

Suz was a new client of mine, and her presenting problem was that she felt abnormally sad and alone in life. She was nearing thirty, had a solid job, and was single. Singleness was not something that had really started to bother her until recently. Ever since graduating from college she'd had a close-knit group of friends consisting of both married couples and singles. They would gather on the weekends for a bite to eat, work out together, or meet up for coffee. In the past year, however, all of Suz's close single friends had become engaged or gotten married, and the couples had started having babies.

Suz was left feeling like the only single in a sea of young married couples. To make things worse, when she left church on Sundays she felt like she had to scramble to find lunch plans. The newlyweds were headed home to save money and work on DIY projects, while the older married couples had to wrangle their newborns down for naps.

She longed for a partner to share life with, but every guy she had dated up to this point was not right for her. She found herself wanting to wave the white flag and stop trying. When Suz slumped down on my sofa, she looked up at me with her hazel eyes and asked, "What do you think is wrong with me?"

Why is this the first place we go in our minds when we feel like we are overlooked? Why do we blame our circumstances on how we do or don't measure up? What if what we want in the moment is simply not God's best for us right now? Do we believe he is protecting us from hurt?

A few years ago I read an article by the vibrant Annie Downs in which she talked about being reduced to tears one Sunday while attending church in the morning and a concert in the evening.[9] She writes how there were empty seats to either side of her at the beginning of each event, and she found herself throwing a pity party because of how alone she felt in both places. Not once, however, but twice in that one day God ended up filling those seats with some of her favorite people, reminding her that he sees her and is with her in her singleness.

Manna for the moment. God gave Annie just what her heart desired, *sacred connection.*

We all crave connection. It's not something we can escape in this life because of the way God knit us together in our mother's womb. We are relational beings and God gave us these desires.

So when I sit with women like Suz who are asking the question "What is wrong with me?" I like to reframe that negative thought into a positive and true belief that their desire is good. Longing to be connected to people, specifically a future spouse, can be a God-given dream. Shaming ourselves for wanting to fulfill a desire he put within us is harmful and leaves us restless.

So as my session with Suz ended that day, we agreed that she would spend the next few weeks asking God which relationships she should intentionally deepen in her life. Instead of looking around at what she didn't have or beating herself up for even wanting connection in the first place, she would try *uncovering what relationships were already around her* and deeply investing in those. Instead of trying to go about it in her own strength, she needed God to help her discover the manna in her midst that she hadn't been able to see before. She also agreed to carve out some time to sit with Jesus in the mystery of it all.

Moses told the Israelites to be still, and I love how Sue Monk Kidd reminds us, "Be still and cooperate with the mystery God is unfolding in you. Let it be."[10]

We don't have to have an answer for all the things.

Can we all just take a collective breath and let that concept of cooperating with the mystery sink in for a moment? We don't have to have an answer for all the things. We can just wonder.

Be Still

As a culture, we are not successful when it comes to stillness. For example, yesterday I was driving through our tiny town and about 95 percent of the people I saw had their head down looking at their phone. While I was stopped at a red light, I even saw one guy jogging while pushing his baby in a stroller, exercising his dog, and holding his phone in his hand. I must admit I was impressed at first glance, but then I started to think about the *impact*. Every choice we make has a cost. I thought about the baby in the stroller, who thrives on interpersonal connection for attachment. I imagined how her dad might engage with her differently if his phone were tucked away during their run. I started to hear in my mind the way he might narrate their surroundings by being present. How he might note the birds chirping in the trees and say her name to get her attention and tell her he loves her with a twinkle in his eye and a smile on his lips. Then the red light turned green, and I put down my phone, on which I had been quickly checking my text messages—something I had just done minutes before.

Because of that baby—and because of the people in my life who I may be silently ignoring—I finally decided to use the *downtime settings* in my iPhone's new Screen Time feature. In today's world, we all have a problem sitting still and letting our minds rest. We are exchanging the wonder and beauty of our surroundings for a flashy light on a box in our hands.

In a recent CNN article, an Apple CEO admitted that he opens his phone a whopping seventy-five times a day according to the new Screen Time tracking feature on his iPhone X. The article continues, "Rosen says his research shows that young adults spend about five hours a day on their devices and glance at them 50 to 60 times. A survey from Deloitte put that figure at 47 times daily."[11] We have an obvious problem, a compulsion that many of us have been swept up in for a decade now. And it's not going to get better any time soon unless we are intentional with our time and what we see.

So what does it look like to stand at the edge of the sea, or at the forefront of our lives, overwhelmed by all that is around us, and choose to do as Moses says and just *be still*?

I practice this with clients in my office every day, since it is a carved-out time for us to be present together for fifty minutes. I put my phone on silent and out of view before every session begins, and I take the ten minutes I have between sessions to sit in stillness. It is a spiritual discipline I have put in place to re-center and empty myself so God can fill me up before I enter into the sacred stories of my clients. I can tell a drastic difference if I don't do this.

Once my client enters my office, I intentionally try not to fill the space and silence with noise. I let them guide the start of our conversation, and at some point we will usually circle back around to stillness. You can implement this into your daily life as well. My granddaddy Ellis always said that you are late if you are not ten minutes early. I think he was ahead of his time in knowing what society needs to slow down our pace. Imagine if everywhere you went you arrived ten minutes early. What if you allowed yourself those ten minutes to sit in your car or in the waiting room and just breathe? Imagine how your whole being might function if you did this. To protect us, God designed our brains to recalibrate and recharge after any time of rest.

>> **What would it take for you to intentionally create times of stillness in your rhythm of life?**

> » Do you need to adjust the downtime setting on your phone, leave for work earlier, or walk instead of drive to create some margin and quiet in your day to be more attuned to God?

> » Pay attention to how you feel when you sit still without scrolling. Write about what emotions or compulsions rise up in you.

Being mindful of our body and listening to what we need is not a selfish act. It is similar to when a flight attendant instructs passengers to put on their own oxygen mask first before helping the person beside them in the event of an emergency. We desperately need to reclaim these moments throughout our day to calm our limbic system and allow our prefrontal cortex to form logical thoughts before we just react in fight or flight. God made us this way.

For example, when two of my three kids were in diapers, I was getting to the point of overwhelm. I had a song by Ellie Holcomb on my playlist that was based on Psalm 103, and every time I had to perform that messy, mundane task of changing a diaper, I stilled my heart by listening to Ellie sing *words of truth* over my soul.

You don't have to come up with some extravagant plan to incorporate stillness into your life. Sometimes all it takes is a few deep breaths and an extra ten minutes. Simply sit and relax your body from head to toe, and inhale and exhale to a count of five. You'll be amazed at how rejuvenated your soul feels. The benefits will far outweigh anything semiproductive you could do in that time.

Someone to Sing About

Music has always been something that makes me feel alive. I've never been able to pinpoint when I first found it as a simultaneous balm for my heartache and release for my joy, because it just feels like it's always been a part of who I am. I used to spend hours up in our music room, where my dad, who was a DJ, had his fancy speakers and all his albums displayed for me to explore. When I was in elementary school, I would disappear for the afternoon and listen to everything from U2 to Joni Mitchell. I would sing at the top of my lungs and dance freely.

The inner workings of our soul must be set free somehow. It looks different for everyone based on our personalities and seasons of life. When I was little, music was my heartbeat, and it has followed me into adulthood and recently been reawakened in ways I did not expect. We simply can't escape the intricate features of how we were knit together; they always resurface.

When the Israelites made their way through the Red Sea and looked back in awe at all God had done, *their instinct was to sing*. In his comments on Exodus 15, Desmond Alexander writes,

> In the light of everything that God had done for them, the Israelites fittingly worship him in song. . . . This celebration does not dwell simply on the past. The song looks with optimism to the future, anticipating the settlement of the Israelites in the land of Canaan. . . . This is an indication that the exodus is about much more than setting slaves free. It is about the harmonious relationship between God and those redeemed from bondage to evil.[12]

It is important to note the foreshadowing here in Exodus to the rescue we experience when Jesus dies on the cross and breaks the chain of captivity once and for all. The grander narrative is beginning to come into clearer focus at this point of our journey. Throughout each story in Exodus, we can hear the *echoes of Jesus's love* and see glimpses of his rescue plan. I love how Sally Lloyd-Jones calls God the Great Rescuer.[13] Rescue births praise.

At the edge of the Red Sea, as we see God protecting his people, Moses and Miriam sing the first song recorded in the Bible, and all of Israel joins in! In Exodus 15:1–21 they sing, "The LORD is my strength and my song" and "The LORD will reign forever and ever" (ESV), and then they victoriously recount all that God has done to deliver them. We are compelled to worship because we were made for it.

When it feels like the waves of life are going to consume us, we have a clear choice. We can look back on our stories and be bound by the darkness, letting it take root and defeat us, or we can sing a song of hope that springs us forward in the middle of the mess and points to God's protection and provision. The prophet Isaiah summarizes this beautifully when he says,

> Forget the former things;
>   do not dwell on the past.
> See, I am doing a new thing!
>   Now it springs up; do you not perceive it?
> I am making a way in the wilderness
>   and streams in the wasteland. (Isa. 43:18–19)

May we be people who can take a courageous look back at our stories and with God's help and the support of our community find the manna in our midst and *sing out in worship*.

May we point back to our Protector, as he has rescued us from the grip of fearing our enemy, and release the tension we hold over to our Rescuer.

1. Have you ever experienced a time when deep doubt took root in your life? If so, where did you seek comfort to prevent the waves from consuming you? Can you retrace parts of your story where you can see how God has served as your protector?

2. Is there something in life that you are longing for but that feels out of your reach? Journal about what you are really craving behind that desire and *name those dreams.*

3. What keeps you from being still? How often do you find yourself grabbing your phone during any given day? Try putting your phone out of sight and out of reach for ten minutes today. Use that time to inhale and exhale, and wait to hear from God in the stillness. Write about how you felt before, during, and after your still moments.

4. What makes you come alive and what keeps you from experiencing full life? Is it fear? Insecurity? Comparison? Despair?

5. Looking back at your childhood, what is something
   that has been tucked away in you for years but
   is bubbling to the surface? What is God stirring
   up in your heart today that he may be calling you
   towards?

re:sound

"Red Sea Road" by Ellie Holcomb

bread + water

I AM FILLED

In the desert the whole community grumbled against Moses and Aaron. The Israelites said to them, "If only we had died by the LORD's hand in Egypt! There we sat around pots of meat and ate all the food we wanted, but you have brought us out into this desert to starve this entire assembly to death."

Exodus 16:2–3

"What gives moments meaning is not the moments themselves but the presence of Christ with us in the midst of them."

—Emily P. Freeman

thirteen

THE ISRAELITES HAD LEFT the familiar behind and embarked on a journey with very few details and no GPS to follow. They most likely felt out of control and afraid. Just the thought of sore feet, a grumbling stomach, and having to trust a man I hardly know to guide me blindly through a desert with no end in sight breeds anxiety for me. Honestly, I tend to trust myself more than I trust other people, so this would not have been a walk in the park for me.

As they began their long trek to the promised land, the people started to feel thirsty and hungry. They were quick to complain out of a desperation we feel when we are not sure how our basic needs will be met. The people had shifted their eyes away from what life looked like in captivity and toward their own bellies. The way they *felt* was erasing their memory of all God had done up to this point. I imagine it was something like when my blood sugar starts dipping too low and I begin impulsively saying irrational things.

The Bible says:

> Then Moses led Israel from the Red Sea and they went into the Desert of Shur. For three days they traveled in the desert

without finding water. When they came to Marah, they could not drink its water because it was bitter. So the people grumbled against Moses, saying, "What are we to drink?" (Exod. 15:22–24)

God provided for them by turning the water from bitter to sweet. He reminded them that if they would follow him, he would provide what they needed along their path.[1] They just had to trust. But it wasn't long before the Israelites were ranting again—this time about how hungry they were:

The LORD said to Moses, "I have heard the grumbling of the Israelites. Tell them, 'At twilight you will eat meat, and in the morning you will be filled with bread. Then you will know that I am the LORD your God.'" (16:11–12)

When they woke up the next morning they had their first encounter with tangible manna. I imagine them stumbling out of their tents, a bit disoriented and sore from the previous night's slumber. Gazing out over the ground near and far, they saw an unfamiliar frosty substance covering the earth. It was mysterious in form, like nothing they had seen before, and they stood in awe, looking to Moses for their next move.

God said he had heard their cries and would provide what they needed, and now *here it was*.

But they asked, "What is it?" (16:15).

As I mentioned earlier, the word *manna* simply means "what is it?" God's provision is full of mystery and requires an element of trust we are not always willing to lean into. We have been tracing the hand of God not only through the Exodus story but also in our own stories. We have looked at some of my clients' stories and seen them asking "what is it?" while desperately hunting for the hidden manna. Now we get a glimpse into what it was like for the Israelites to hold God's tangible provision *in their hands*. Can you imagine what that must have felt like?

In our humanity our trust expands when we can hold on to what we have been hoping for.

You might feel a bit like the Israelites wandering around in a land of longing and despair.

You might feel like you are fumbling around in the dark, wondering why your life looks like it does or why you feel the way you do.

You might be turning over every rock to find some relief.

You might be hungering and thirsting for something that will last in a world where it feels like everything is fleeting.

We all have something we *want*. We all *hunger*.

It's mid-October as I write this, and here in the southern states we seem to have jumped straight from summer to winter. As I bundled up my kids and ushered them out of the house beneath dark skies on our way to school, I peered over the field next to our gravel drive and discovered the first frost of the year. The kids instantly started squealing, as if it was the only time they had ever seen this white blanket over the earth.

They proceeded to run over to absorb the beauty with wild abandon and delight. *Their wonder* at the frozen dew was a gift to behold! Our oldest was hesitant, not wanting to step on it and get his shoes wet. Our middle child was already holding a handful and shoving it into his mouth by the time

I made my way over. Our youngest had a twinkle in her eye that I just wanted to bottle up, and a question hovered on the tip of her tongue: *What is it?*

When the Ways of This World Don't Satisfy

Jane's mom called me in early January, a time when I get an influx of calls from people wanting to experience more whole living in the New Year. She told me over the phone that she didn't know how to help her sixteen-year-old daughter, who she believed was battling an eating disorder. She had noticed a pattern when Jane would go days without eating, then binge on anything within reach in their kitchen. She would then hear Jane vomiting in the bathroom and flushing the toilet repeatedly. She knew that as a mom, there were only so many times she could tell Jane that she thought she was beautiful. She wanted Jane to believe it for herself and thought counseling might help her gain some hope.

I will never forget the day Jane walked into my office. She wrapped her thin arm around the first seat she could find and slowly slipped into the pale blue antique chair. I could tell by her sunken-in cheeks and the way her jeans were falling off her hips that she was not healthy. She looked up at me with a weariness that revealed her hunger and thirst, then proceeded to tell me her story.

Jane said that it had started out subtly a few years earlier, when her hormones had kicked in and her curves had developed. A guy in her biology class had made some demeaning comments. All summer long her self-absorbed friends spent every day commenting on their bodies at the pool where Jane hung out. She started to limit her calories and overexercise to attain the body she wanted. Her standard for what she desired to look like came from Instagram and Pinterest images. Since it seemed like all the girls at school who had flat stomachs were happy, Jane's goal was to do the same. The only problem was that she quickly became stuck in a cycle of bulimia. Food became less of an enjoyment and more of a need so she could function—it was a means to an end so she could look a certain way. She found herself compulsively eating after restricting, then getting sick and not being able to keep anything in her stomach.

Our desire to look and feel a certain way starts young and can haunt us throughout life unless we find a *healthy way of managing our body image* and the way we view food. So the first thing we have to do when we are trying to satisfy our cravings is to go beneath the surface and ask *What do I really want?*

The resounding answer is always, *To be accepted and known and loved as I am.*

It takes awhile to reach that point in therapy, but once we do, the gates are wide open toward healing. Once we can name what we are really craving, food loses its power and we can learn to be more comfortable in our own skin. Giving in to the compulsions and cravings slowly ceases.

Craving Enough in a Land of Longing

Enough.

We want to *have enough* and we want to *be enough*, especially when we have had enough already.

We have all repeated these phrases in one way or another throughout our time together in this book.

Let's do a quick review:

The Israelites had their basic needs met in the midst of
  slavery.

God met them in their desperation during the trauma of
  hard labor.

God provided a way out when there seemed to be no
  way in Egypt.

Tribe by tribe they entered into freedom *together,* so they
  didn't have to do it alone.

God showed up in the form of fire and cloud to guide
  them through the desert.

The people had peace when they cried out in doubt and
  fear on the journey.

God hemmed them in behind and before as they crossed
  through the Red Sea.

God turned bitter water sweet and provided manna and
  quail to satisfy their hunger and thirst.

After each provision, the Israelites felt seen, known, and
loved. Although they'd had to be patient and trust God, he had
come through for them. His provision hardly ever looked the
way they thought it would, but they were always provided for.

However, when they came to the next obstacle, they quickly
forgot how God had provided in even the heaviest of circumstances. All they could see was the immediate pain or need.
They found themselves back in the same place, blind to the
gifts right in front of them: *the breath they were breathing, the community in their corner, and the provision
on the way.* Again they doubted and often wondered if they

had been overlooked or forgotten by God. They cried out repeatedly, *Where does my help come from? How will we survive this? Will I yearn forever?*

Doesn't it seem maddening, this back and forth cycle of trust followed quickly by distrust?

You might experience the same wavering in your own life on a regular basis. But I hope that you have also tasted the manna of *heaven meeting earth* in your own life. The reality is that you and I cannot wave a magic wand and fix all the things we want to. Sometimes things are just too broken and seem beyond repair. We cannot do it in our own strength, but we do know One who can bring calm into the chaos. The circumstances might not change but our mind-set can. We have a God who wants to wrap us up in his canopy of comfort; to fill us up to the brim with a love that overflows out of his abundant provision in this life.

> » Where is God revealing himself in your life in both
> tangible and intangible ways?

> » Take some time to look at a few areas of your life
> and make a list of the provision you have seen.

When we become mindful of where we are in the moment, we give ourselves permission to be present in the here and now. So often we look ahead and make plans and think we can make it all happen. If only we could sit still for a second and relish the reality of *now*, we might grasp how loved and filled up we already are. If we could look back at all that has happened in our past, then maybe we could more easily have hope for what is to come. We all share in the heartache of life's unpredictable disappointments, yet we share in the radiant joys too. If our lens could shift and we could start to see God's hand bringing light into the dark, maybe we could begin to trust him more, even in our heaviest and hardest seasons.

What if our eyes shifted from what we need to what we already hold in our hands?

> » If you were to hold out your hands right now, what would you list as manna in your life?
>
> » Are your hands starting to fill up? How does this shift your perspective?
>
> » How can you wake up to this reality more often in your everyday coming and going?

We have seen God at work in the stories of the women and men who have sat on my couch. At first it may have seemed like he was absent from their lives, but the reality is that he was close by, carrying them through it all. Their hands are *full*.

Surveying the Scene

As we have traced the hand of our Creator in the Exodus narrative, from Israel's slavery in Egypt and out into the desolate wilderness, we have seen his provision unfolding time after time.

We have also observed a forgetful people, who continually ache for relief just moments after each need is supplied.

We zoomed into the narrative of the Israelites when they were living under the reign of an oppressive pharaoh who forced them into hard labor.

We saw both the Israelites and the Egyptians stand in awe of God's power when he brought the ten plagues upon the land.

We watched God fight for his people when he instructed them to put the blood of the Passover lamb on their doorposts so the angel of death would pass over those households.

What if our eyes shifted from what we need to what we already hold in our hands?

We watched as God's people fled from their oppressors and entered an unknown wilderness. We saw God guide his stubborn people in the form of a cloud by day and a pillar of fire by night.

When there seemed to be no way through the Red Sea with the enemy on their heels, we saw God make a way.

We watched Pharaoh's army get swept into the sea as the Israelites marched safely through on dry ground.

We saw God meet his people in their thirsty groaning, and he turned bitter water into the sweet refreshment they needed in that moment.

We saw God's people consider going back into slavery because it was more predictable and comfortable than their newfound freedom, which felt risky and out of their control.

Now we see God responding to their cries that they are tired and hungry from their desert travels. In looking back at what they had left behind and looking ahead to what they did not yet hold in their hands, the Israelites were left aching in the in-between. They doubted. They wondered whether they would actually reach their homeland before they starved to death. So God provided by raining down this bizarre substance called manna.[2] The psalmist Asaph recalled this when he wrote, "He rained down on them manna to eat and gave them the grain of heaven. Man ate of the bread of the angels; he sent them food in abundance . . . and they ate and were well filled, for he gave them what they craved" (Ps. 78:24–25, 29 ESV).

Why manna?

The Israelites were told not to store up any of the manna but to only gather what they needed each day. For the duration of their desert journey, they were expected to trust that every day God would provide *enough*. For those who didn't listen and gathered extra, their stash of manna rotted overnight and was crawling with maggots.[3]

I have a tendency to think that I know best, so I imagine that I would have been one of the hoarders. I would have tried to sneak a few extra baskets full of manna, just in case what God had promised didn't actually happen. My lack of faith tends to slip into pride. I like to think that if I do things my way, then I will get the outcome I long for. We've seen how this usually turns out.

At first the Israelites must have appreciated this flaky, edible dew that God provided when they were desperate for food. But based on their history, you can imagine that eating the same thing for forty years would cause some complaining.[4] God knew what they needed before they even cried out to him, and he began providing *quail* in the evening. Despite all their meanderings and distrust, God had compassion on his people. His kindness and love were evident in the hundreds of ways he provided for them throughout their journey from slavery to the promised land.

God's love for us is unconditional too. He does not keep a record of wrongs—he anticipates our needs.

fourteen

SOMETIMES IT IS SO OBVIOUS when God is lavishing his love on us. I see it in my own life when a *friend* shows up right when I need them. Or when I walk into a bookstore and a *timely title* stares me down as if to say, *I've been waiting for you to walk in here and pick me up.* Or when my husband *says just what I need to hear* if I am doubting myself and can't seem to finish up a project. I hear God's lavish love when *my son sings a song* from the depths of his soul and the lyrics breathe hope into what I am battling right then and there. Sometimes that love comes tangibly in the form of *a check that arrives in the mail* when the monthly budget is tight and a dear friend just felt like the Lord was telling them to share their excess with our family.

My list could go on and on. It is all manna. Gifts of provision that we sometimes don't even know we need.

> » Look back at the list you journaled in chapter 13
> and survey the manna moments in your life. Now
> take some more time to write about the context
> leading up to the provision God gave you.

Manna-filled moments flow all day long. Heaven is meeting earth with every single one.

Yet we can be blind to God's good gifts because we focus on what isn't working right now and how hopeless we feel in our day-to-day life. At times we refuse to see his provision right here in front of us; all we see is what we lack.

Manna-filled moments flow all day long. Heaven is meeting earth with every single one.

When we are continually focused on the pain we feel, moving out of it doesn't happen easily. There are times we need to sit in our pain and really explore why we feel the way we do. We need to take the time to grieve thoroughly and find healing, and the length of that process is different for everyone. We need to come to terms with the world's brokenness. We need to be reminded of how God brings beauty out of the broken places and stop blaming him and the people around us. We need to trust harder and rest in the arms of our Creator. We need to hash it out with the Lord like the prophet Jeremiah did:

> I remember my affliction and my wandering,
>   the bitterness and the gall.
> I well remember them,
>   and my soul is downcast within me.
> Yet this I call to mind
>   and therefore I have hope:
> Because of the LORD's great love we are not
>   consumed,
>   for his compassions never fail.
> They are new every morning;
>   great is your faithfulness.

I say to myself, "The LORD is my portion;
therefore I will wait for him." (Lam. 3:19–24)

If we look back at the manna God provided for the Israelites in the wilderness, we can clearly see that he never abandoned them. He was always near. But somehow when it comes to our own need for daily bread and sustenance, we think he has removed himself or chosen to let us suffer for a little while—or maybe forever. We are an entitled people. We have so much that whenever something doesn't go our way, we feel like we have nothing. By considering the manna God provided daily for the Israelites, we can slowly begin to trust God with the modern-day manna he provides for us too. It's simply a matter of searching for his hand.

We could just stop right here and give thanks for all the provision God lavished on his people as they waited and wandered in the desert and for the ways he sends various forms of modern-day manna to each of us. But we would be settling for less than the abundance God has in mind. See, the Israelites were getting the sustenance they needed every day, but the reality is that eventually their bodies would still return to the dust from which they came.

Although we are provided generous gifts of grace throughout our lifetime, such manna moments are not the answer to the bigger need we all must face. Each earthly form of manna can only offer us so much.

Jesus—the Son of the God of Abraham, Isaac, Jacob, Joseph, Moses, you, me—is God's greatest provision. He himself said,

I am the bread of life. Your ancestors ate the manna in the wilderness, yet they died. But here is the bread that comes

down from heaven, which anyone may eat and not die. I am
the living bread that came down from heaven. Whoever eats
this bread will live forever. This bread is my flesh, which I will
give for the life of the world. (John 6:48–51)

Jesus is our Manna. Only he can truly satisfy the greater
hunger within our souls. We get so hung up on what we long
for and crave, thinking that will be something we can hold
in our hands, when what we really long for is *Someone we
can carry with us* wherever we go in life.

Jesus came to earth as a baby born of a virgin. He came to
die a brutal death on the cross, where he took on himself all
the aching and sin and pain that we have ever experienced or
ever will experience. "For God so loved the world that he gave
his one and only Son, that whoever believes in him shall not
perish but have eternal life. For
God did not send his Son into the
world to condemn the world, but
to save the world through him"
(John 3:16–17).

Jesus himself is God's ultimate
provision, our Manna. He is everything we long for, and only he can
truly satisfy us and bring us full life.
As he says in John's Gospel, "The
thief comes only to steal and kill
and destroy; I have come that they
may have life, and have it to the full" (John 10:10). We all long
for more on this side of heaven, but our true ache is fulfilled
only in the person of Jesus. He is our hope. When life leaves us
wanting, he leaves us satisfied. He meets us in our brokenness

Although we are provided generous gifts of grace throughout our lifetime, such manna moments are not the answer to the bigger need we all must face.

and offers us his peace. His presence and our connection to him are *more than enough*.

Jesus's sacrifice makes all the difference for our life. He is all we need. He fills us.

The Sweet Surrender

On the day that I fully surrendered my life into the hands of Jesus and deepened my relationship with him, my whole world shifted. The deep ache I felt in my soul began to heal as I became more in tune with the One who knows the hidden places in my heart and loves me anyway. No matter what is happening in and around my little corner of the world, a *deep peace* rises up in my soul as I feel seen and noticed by my Creator. I still don't always understand what is happening, but now I try to step back and see the bigger picture of what God might be up to instead of just focusing on what is right in front of my two feet. I feel satisfaction in knowing that the ache that haunted me for so long stemmed from a condition that was beyond my control. The darkness that entered our world in the garden penetrates our lives today, and although there is no way for us to make it better, we have a rescuer in Jesus, who is our bridge back to God.

The truth is, if I hadn't had that moment of surrender, I'd still be attempting to live life on my own, out of my own strength. I still have anxiety that likes to rear its ugly head at times, and yet I sit here in awe of God's provision and presence through every ounce of my pain.

Know this: *Although many of us have a relationship with Jesus, we might also continue battling anxiety.*

At times we might feel like we are unable to tap into the peace that he offers, simply because we think we can handle life on our own. We may go back and forth, trying to regain control of our life and live it on our terms. But I'm confident that on this side of heaven anxiety is a persistent thorn because the enemy knows it is a highly effective tool he can use against us. He knows that when we feel weak, he can whisper lies to us. He wants us to listen to him instead of to the One who made us. Just as he deceived Eve in the garden, the enemy tries to convince us that God is holding out on us. In this struggle, we let those lies take root and we start to believe a false script that is scary and just plain untrue. But I personally know how real it can feel.

All humanity is guilty of believing lies instead of truth. Lies separate us from the gospel, which says that all our efforts *will* fail but that what we need has already been done for us by Jesus on the cross. When the lies feel overwhelming, we can remember again the words of Isaiah: "Do not fear, for I have redeemed you; I have summoned you by name; you are mine. When you pass through the waters, I will be with you; and when you pass through the rivers, they will not sweep over you" (Isa. 43:1–2).

So when the anxiety of this life comes around—and we all know it will—may we learn to let it come in and sit with us for a while. May we remember that God holds the ultimate power and surrender it all over to him. May we loosen our grip and let him fill us up with himself.

It is all about surrender.

Abundant life is found in the sweet surrender, in the letting go.

1. What does it look like for you to embrace both peace and pain?

2. Where do you see modern-day manna in your life? In others' lives?

3. How have you experienced Jesus as the ultimate Manna in your life?

4. Take some time to read over Psalm 23 and reflect on what it says to you. I've included it here in the New King James Version.

> The LORD is my shepherd;
> I shall not want.
> He makes me to lie down in green pastures;
> He leads me beside the still waters.
> He restores my soul;
> He leads me in the paths of righteousness
> For His name's sake.
> Yea, though I walk through the valley of the shadow of death,
> I will fear no evil;
> For You are with me;
> Your rod and Your staff, they comfort me.
> You prepare a table before me in the presence of my enemies;
> You anoint my head with oil;
> My cup runs over.
> Surely goodness and mercy shall follow me

All the days of my life;
And I will dwell in the house of the LORD
Forever.

5. How is God specifically calling you to surrender to
   him in your life today?

re:sound

"I Shall Not Want" by Audrey Assad

etched in stone

I AM SECURED

Indeed we have all received grace upon grace from his fullness, for the law was given through Moses; grace and truth came through Jesus Christ.

John 1:16–17 CSB

"You come to God not by being strong, but by being weak; not by being right, but through your mistakes."

—Richard Rohr

fifteen

MOSES HAD JUST LED the Israelites through the Wilderness of Sin to camp in a place where there was no water. Once again God's people complained of thirst, and once again God provided *the water* they needed, this time from a rock.[1] This is yet another foreshadowing of Jesus, the Rock from whom living water flows.

The next bump in the road came in the form of Amalek and his army. As Joshua, Moses's right-hand man, led Israel's forces, God enabled Israel to defeat the army by sending his power through the *outstretched arms of Moses,* which were being supported by Aaron and Hur. Once again God defeated the enemy ahead of the Israelites in the camp. They built an altar that they called "The Lord Is My Banner" as a reminder of God's faithfulness to his people to always defeat the enemy that is looking to harm.[2]

Finally, Moses led the Israelites to the foot of Mount Sinai. Jethro, Moses's father-in-law, met them there and was amazed to hear how God had delivered Israel out of Egypt and provided all their needs along the journey. He stood in awe and *became a believer* in the God of Israel.[3] After giving Moses some advice on how to delegate his responsibilities to help sustain him for the long haul, Jethro returned to his land and Moses made his first trek up Mount Sinai.

It is important to pause here and zoom out. Not only was Jethro personally being redeemed by God and becoming grafted into the family of Israel because of his belief, but anyone today can do the same. The only requirement to find redemption and enter into a relationship with God is to believe he is who he says he is and to walk in the way of the Lord, which we will soon see unfold. It was through stories of God's grander narrative that Jethro joined in. He simply could not resist being part of something that was attractive and fulfilling. From the outside looking in he could tell that the God of Israel stood out, and their story moved him.

Claire bounced into my office with a shiny ring on her finger. She and her fiancé Jack had recently been engaged and came to me for premarital counseling. They were in their late twenties and had met just six months earlier through mutual friends at church. They both came from mostly stable families who were well known in our community.

After spending a month delving deep into their stories, we were about to begin our final session. But I could sense that Jack was holding something back. He had been darting his eyes at me since their first visit. Claire was a hopeless romantic and had fallen head over heels for Jack on their first date. She could barely see for all the stars in her eyes. Jack clearly loved Claire too, but there was something subtle I could not put my finger on. Jack traveled a lot for his job, and in this session I decided to ask each of them to voice their expectations about the amount of time they would spend together after they were married.

Claire quickly responded with excitement about making meals together and hosting their community group at their house once a week. Jack's mind seemed to spin when he realized how full his calendar already was on weeknights, and he started shifting in his seat. I asked Jack if that sounded feasible with his current job, and for some reason he wouldn't look me in the eye. Unsettled, Claire laughed off the way he was reacting, even as I repeated the question for him.

Out of nowhere Jack snapped, "I don't think I can do this!" I caught Claire's eye and she instantly started weeping. There was an elephant in the room and it seemed I was the only one who needed an explanation. Jack stood up straight in his slim-fit suit and started fumbling around for his keys as if he needed to leave.

I asked Jack to sit down and told them both to take a breath so we could uncover what was really going on.

Claire proceeded to divulge what she had discovered on Jack's iPad the previous evening when she was looking up something for their wedding vendor. In looking through the browsing history to find the link she needed, Claire had stumbled upon some websites that Jack had been looking at nightly for months. After clicking on a few of them, she called him into the room and began asking questions. Jack's first response was to blame his roommate, but that lie was quickly exposed when Claire reminded him that earlier she had needed his password to get on the iPad herself. So here we sat, the three of us, in the final session of premarital counseling, with the groom ready to walk away and the bride ready to walk forward and tuck it all under the rug.

We all agreed that our work together was not done, and they decided to keep coming on a weekly basis leading up to the wedding. For Jack, addiction ran in his family, and a year earlier he had been in rehab for alcohol and drug dependency. He rediscovered his faith through the *12-step program*, as many addicts do, and found a church and community to come alongside him in this new season. Just months later he met Claire. After they got engaged, Jack found himself craving his old ways again. His solution was to pretend like everything was fine, and instead of reaching out for help, he quickly picked up his old habit of watching pornography.

The beautiful part of Claire and Jack's story is that their relationship didn't end there. They continued attending sessions even after the wedding and are still happily married. Jack is fully aware of his need for *extra support*, and Claire loves him deeply. They each recognize that in their own way they are in need of a Savior every day, and they both want God's best.

Astray

Our tendency as a culture is to look around and see all the brokenness in the world and not see it in ourselves. I hear parents talking about how the kids of the world have lost their sense of manners, and I watch husbands and wives treat each other like they are not worthy of love. I see families eating out at restaurants while both parents are on their cell phones. I see young women bash their friends on social media and moms judging each other in Target. This is all for public consumption, so we can only imagine what is happening behind closed doors.

The truth is that none of us are living pure and blameless lives. The prophet Isaiah says, "We all, like sheep, have gone astray, each of us has turned to our own way; and the LORD has laid on him the iniquity of us all" (Isa. 53:6).

So what would it be like to stop looking at all the brokenness around us and uncover what lies beneath the surface of our own lives? What is behind the facade we put up?

> » If someone were to take a long look at your life behind closed doors, what would they find? What just popped into your mind?

> » Are you struggling to bring your burdens into the light before God or your trusted people? If you were to lay it all out, what would you find and could you justify its presence? Or is it time to let it go?

Our *stories* of how God has met us in our life also have lasting impact on those we love. In telling our stories we remember all God has done and will continue to do. Sometimes when we are unable to see, hearing others' stories resurrects our hope.

Every example of God's provision in the desert and deliverance from the enemy is an echo of his love in manna form. However, when we are in the midst of a dry season, we can't always see the big picture. As Alec Motyer comments, "The Lord works to a larger pattern than we can see at any given point."[4]

If we put ourselves in the sandals of Moses and the Israelites, it is easy to understand why they kept groaning. Even though they were out of Egypt, in many ways they were still feeling the effects of the oppression they had experienced. At this point they were still a long way from the land they had been promised and were taking many detours and enduring many battles.

Motyer continues by reminding us what a gift we have in the *Bible*, our own form of manna that we get to hold in our hands and consume word by word, day by day:

> As for us with the Bible in our hands and helped by hindsight, everything is explained, for what we have here is in fact the largest, most extended visual aid ever planned: the journey from the Passover in Egypt to the giving of the Law at Sinai. . . . The Lord's redeemed people had to be brought to the place where they could hear and receive his law. The grace of God precedes the law.[5]

Like the shower analogy I shared in chapter 11, we are reminded that we do not have to try to clean ourselves off before we come to God. We can simply rest in his grace. This is our grounding that helps us have a firm foundation.

After Jethro left, Israel camped at the foot of Mount Sinai for a year. In that time, Moses made his way up the mountain not once, but seven times.[6] There was clearly a lot to be established between God and his people about what it looks like to live according to God's will on earth.

Moses's first few ascents up the mountain were a preparation, as God was intentionally *taking his time* to earn the right to be heard with his people. We would like to think their hearts were primed and ready to hear anything he had to say by this point, but they weren't. Only after God had revealed enough about his nature and Moses had prepared the people did he give them the *Ten Commandments*. At the strike of lightning and the sound of thunder, the Israelites pleaded for Moses to be their mediator with God.[7] God's people trembled in his presence because his power is so profound that they couldn't handle it. In fear they sent Moses up the mountain to continue the conversation with God.

> » Can you relate? Has there been a time in your life when you have felt as if simply being near God might level you?

I wonder if our desire to keep a distance has less to do with God and more to do with what we carry. What if the reason we don't want to get too close has to do with the condition of our hearts and the dark things we don't want to be exposed? Whatever it may be, it's essential to note that even when we withdraw, God lovingly approaches us. Just as he came down to the level of the Israelites, he meets us right where we are too. He secures us in his mercy instead of isolating us on the shaky ground we stand on.

He secures us in his mercy instead of isolating us on the shaky ground we stand on.

At this point in our journey together, we can clearly understand the kind of life that God is calling his people to live. In our insecurity, we may find ourselves wanting to slam this book shut just as the Israelites wanted to hide. Maybe you are afraid of judgment or of not being able to live up to God's expectations. Perhaps your fear is winning. Let's take a moment to look at the commandments and see how we measure up. In Exodus 20:3–17, God commanded Israel:

1. Do not have other gods before me.
2. Do not make an idol for yourself.
3. Do not misuse the name of the Lord your God.
4. Remember the Sabbath day, to keep it holy.
5. Honor your father and your mother.
6. Do not murder.
7. Do not commit adultery.
8. Do not steal.
9. Do not give dishonest testimony against your neighbor.
10. Do not covet.

If I had been standing there that day, I would have felt overwhelmed by this list. Honestly, even today it overwhelms me. In some way, shape, or form we have all fallen short.[8]

When We Want to Run and Hide

Sin is anything that separates us from God. And if we're honest with ourselves about our sin condition, we'll admit that we need *help*. It goes all the way back to the garden and follows us to the grave. We're in great need of a Savior, someone who can rescue us from the mess we've made. It is understandable that all we want to do is run and hide! Yet Paul reminds us in Romans 10 that "Anyone who believes in him will never be put to shame" (v. 11) and that "Everyone who calls on the name of the Lord will be saved" (v. 13).

This is the gospel in a nutshell. To me this is the best part of the Exodus story because it all points back to Jesus being our ultimate Manna. It's what the whole narrative is about—*God's love* being poured out for his people Israel. *Without the law, Israel would not know their need for him.* Without wandering around in our own deserts and battling the enemy, we would not know how desperately we need Someone to rescue us.

When I think back over my own story or the stories of my clients and friends, we are all saying the same thing: this world is too much to bear, and we are weak. But when we are weak, our God is strong.[9] Where we are flawed, our Rescuer is enough. He puts our feet on solid ground.

Where we are flawed, our Rescuer is enough.

But what if we think we are too far gone?

This is a valid question. It takes me right back to that counseling session with Claire and Jack. In that moment when Jack stood up to leave the room, he felt unworthy of the love of his future bride. He was beyond embarrassed and full of shame for the addiction he was battling behind the scenes. To take it a step further, he felt like he was not worthy of God's love.

When we feel exposed, we tend to reach a point in life that can either shift us to shame or freedom. We have a choice whether to walk down the old path of slavery or a new path of healing.

sixteen

IN HIS BOOK *THE SOUL OF SHAME,* Curt Thompson talks about how we are all pilgrims on a journey. I love that image. We are not in the business of pointing fingers at faults but on a journey together to unearth the *goodness* amid our own stories. Curt writes:

Although it is tempting to hope that we can eliminate shame from our relational diet, it is futile to wish for this. Our hope is, rather, changing our response to it as we journey together toward God's kingdom, which is now but not yet in its fullness. We would like to have it excised surgically from our brains, but instead find ourselves having to grow in our confidence in combating it. To do so requires that we strengthen our capacity to turn our attention to something other than shame. As such we do not execute shame quickly via some guillotine, but rather we starve it over time, not by avoiding it but by attuning to it as a component of a larger story. A story whose beginning is as much about how we were made as it is about why we were made.[10]

The goal of looking back at your story is to trace the *hand of God* in your life. My prayer for you, reader, is that you will uncover the root of your hurt. The point is not to resurrect or deepen shame but to set you *free*. By looking at our stories within the context of Exodus, we're able to see our hope that is found in Jesus.

Freedom always comes with a cost; Jesus has already paid it.

While writing this book I stumbled upon a new book titled *Echoes of Exodus* by Alastair Roberts and Andrew Wilson, which looks at how Exodus echoes throughout the entire Bible and in our own lives as well. The authors write, "The greatest threats to true freedom, it seems, do not come from external oppression but from within. . . . True slavery is captivity of the soul, not just the body. Until a nation or person is freed from that, and free to become what they were originally intended to be, their exodus is incomplete."[11]

The greatest threat to true freedom comes from within and holds us back.

The goal of looking back at your story is to trace the hand of God in your life.

The rest of the Israelites' time at the foot of Mount Sinai was spent receiving God's law in great detail. From our view on this side of the cross, we can see that God is not in the business of laying out his law just so people will fail. The whole point of the law is for us to have a way to live in a covenantal relationship with him. God longs for his people to be in a right relationship with him. Jesus fulfilled the law and paid the penalty for our sin so we could be brought back to God, but the Israelites didn't have this revelation just yet.

The law gives us a way to serve and glorify God and find full life—it wakes us up to the fact that, when given in love, parameters and boundaries help us find security here on earth. "Human beings are not designed to be free from all constraint, slaves to nothing but our own gods. Everybody serves somebody. So the point of the exodus is not just for Israel to find deliverance from serving the old master. It is for them to find delight in serving the new one."[12]

If we could really shift our shame to freedom, I believe we would find not only a release from the tight grip of guilt but also the joy that comes from serving our Creator and being grounded by him.

The whole point of the law in the first place is to lead us back to God. He knows us too well to leave us to our own devices. God wanted to set Israel apart from the surrounding culture and establish them as a nation. He also wanted them to experience the fullness of life that comes from the boundaries he sets.

Boundaries are one of the greatest forms of abundant love we can have.

I always thought the word *boundaries* only meant restraint. In college I remember having my understanding transformed after reading the book *Boundaries* by Henry Cloud and John Townsend.[13] The reality is that boundaries are one of the greatest forms of abundant love we can have. Boundaries hem us in for our own security, and we are set apart in our security.

One of my favorite passages is found in Psalm 139: "You hem me in behind and before . . . such knowledge is too wonderful for me, too lofty for me to attain" (vv. 5–6). I love the mystery and truth this *psalm* demonstrates. It's a rich reminder that we cannot fully grasp the ways of the Lord. It is simultaneously humbling and relieving. Instead of viewing the law as a list of things we can't do, what if we saw it as an invitation for living fully? An invitation for finding our footing in a world that would otherwise leave us unstable.

I recently watched a documentary featuring Dan Allender called *The Heart of Man*, which is about the effects of sexual abuse. In the program Dan talked about how we tend to believe God only wants us to conform, when actually he wants to transform us. He says, "If we could only enter the depths of his love, we would find our lives deeply changed."[14]

When we can reach the place where we understand that God sees us even in our darkest moments and loves us anyway, we will find the freedom we crave. Our ache will be eased and we will dance in the *delight and love of our Creator.*

Trusting a Love That Doesn't Make Sense

I admit it isn't always easy to accept that God loves us unconditionally. When life doesn't make sense, it's easier to blame God. After all, isn't he the one in control? Doesn't he hold the whole world in his hands? We have an enemy who prowls like a roaring lion and seeks to devour us.[15] He wants to make us believe that God is holding out on us. He wants us to believe that the law is God's way of making us suffer, and he tempts us to break the law just like he tempted Eve in the garden.

In his book *When God's Way Makes No Sense*, Larry Crabb writes, "Settled, growing trust is required to follow Jesus through every season of life. The needed trust develops only in souls that tremble. We must trust to obey. But we must tremble to trust."[16] We see this shift from trembling to trust as Moses came down from Mount Sinai and brought Israel the Ten Commandments and all the other instructions God had given him. The Bible says, "Then all the people responded with a single voice, 'We will do everything the LORD has commanded'" (Exod. 24:3 CSB). The people agreed to trust and obey God, and in a special ceremony Moses sprinkled all the people with the blood of animal sacrifices as a symbol of the official covenant between them and God.

Animal sacrifice was a necessity in ancient Israel. The price of sin is death.[17] The blood of animals was the temporary means God provided to atone for sin until the day of Jesus's ultimate sacrifice for sin on the cross. Just as the blood of the Passover lamb protected God's people from death during the tenth plague in Egypt, so the blood of sheep and goats and bulls made atonement for their sin.

Moses then ascended the mountain to receive the tablets of the law and get further instructions from God. He remained there in the cloud of God's presence for forty days. Back at camp, however, the people lost their way again and stopped trusting God. *And we all sigh collectively.*

When Moses headed back down the mountain, he found that the Israelites, led by his own brother Aaron, had decided to take matters into their own hands. They broke the first two commandments by making a golden calf to worship, going so far as praising the idol as the god who had delivered them from Egypt.[18]

Idol worship may sound like a thing of the past, yet we do it every day. Anything we put before God becomes an idol, even the good things we accomplish in our life at home and work.

After Moses pleaded with God on behalf of the people, God forgave those who were willing to denounce the calf and follow him again. There would be consequences, but he would not destroy them. Those who chose not to follow him and continued walking their own way experienced God's judgment. Then God renewed his covenant with Israel and gave Moses new stone tablets written by his own hand.

At the end of the day, it's all about trust—for the Israelites and for us. Do we believe that the boundaries God puts around us are for harm or for good? An intentional plan to secure or a plot to withhold?

> » How do you see these conflicting narratives playing out in your life lately?

If we believe and trust, then the prayer that makes the most sense at this point is this:

Search me, God, and know my heart;
    test me and know my anxious thoughts.
See if there is any offensive way in me,
    and lead me in the way everlasting. (Ps. 139:23–24)

God isn't looking to judge us in our darkness. He wants us to invite him into our hidden wounds that hide beneath our visible behaviors. He longs to wade into the rushing waters with us and help heal us from the inside out.

He is always stepping toward us with open hands, ready to be with us in our struggle. We have the freedom to decide whether we want to follow him and trust him. Just as the father welcomed the prodigal son, God welcomes us. May we trust that he loves us.

Amen.

1. Where in your life are you hiding right now? What do you need to bring into the light?

2. How are you currently leaning into the Ten Commandments in your life? What are some boundaries God has given you that are helping you find security?

3. Do shame and guilt have a hold on your life? Do you feel like you fall short? If so, how and why?

4. What is an example of an idol in your life? How is it working for you?

5. Take some time to listen to the song below and journal what comes to mind. What does obedience out of delight look like for you personally?

re:sound

"Come Ye Souls (Look to Jesus)" by Indelible Grace

dwelling place

I AM WITH YOU

They will know that I am the LORD their God, who brought them out of Egypt that I might dwell among them. I am the LORD their God.

Exodus 29:46

"It's strange how that happens—
that any place becomes the
Promised Land when the blessing
of His presence becomes
the gift we receive—and give."

—Ann Voskamp

seventeen

MOSES HAD BEEN LEADING the Israelites through the desert for nearly nine months, and there was no end in sight. I imagine most days felt a little foggy for him as he guided God's people through all the ups and downs. Perhaps he asked himself, *Why did I set out on this journey anyway? Are we ever really going to make it to the promised land? Is God really with us right now?*

We ask ourselves these same questions every day in our own way, especially when it feels like a cloud has been lingering over our life a little longer than we might prefer. We have surveyed many heavy stories throughout our journey together, and the common theme running through all of them has been God's provision and his ability to always bring light into the dark. This is the hope we all are searching for—Someone to join us in the storms of life.

We all crave being with our Maker, who knows us better than we know ourselves.

In our daily life we long for the way things used to be or the way we want things to be—and in the middle of it all we miss out on what is right in front of us. We are blinded to the goodness of the moment because we are too busy looking ahead at what could be or grappling with what we do not yet have. When we feel trapped, stuck in the in-between, we long for our lives to feel more settled, balanced, and secure. We ache for our relationships to be more enjoyable, life-giving, and connected. In an effort to check everything off our list we bypass the beauty right here, right now. Evidence of God's presence and provision abounds if we can just open our eyes to see all the manna around us!

Moment by manna moment, God is showing us that *he is with us* right here, right now, and he is all we really need. He is all our heart desires, and he is the One who satisfies.

In an article from the Allender Center, author Simona Chitescu Weik writes, "So, *to be born again* is to *re-turn* to the expression of humanity that we see in the Garden, dynamic, vulnerable, joyful, worshipful, embodied."[1] In this posture of being mindful to our story while in the presence of Jesus, we get a taste of the glory of the garden as heaven gently meets earth. These are the moments of manna that remind us deep in our bones that God is lavishing us with his love.

I'd just spent the past two hours creeping down the Blue Ridge Parkway in dense fog and heavy rain. After a week alone in the sweeping valley of Banner Elk, North Carolina, writing and resting in a cozy cottage, I had not planned to end my soothing retreat this way. My shoulders were tense, and I felt like I could take a nap for the rest of the year. I was trying to outrun a snowstorm, and my only option was to drive through the fog or get snowed in and be separated from my family for the holidays.

Sometimes life means entering the fog in hopes of finding home on the other side.

As I delved deeper into the mountains the fog grew thicker. I could barely see the guardrail to my right or the car in the lane to my left. The barriers that kept everyone on the road had faded and I was moving along at a snail's pace, holding my breath around each bend. I was listening to one of my favorite hymns, "Abide with Me," and the lyrics brought me to tears:

> Abide with me; fast falls the eventide;
> The darkness deepens; Lord, with me abide;
> When other helpers fail and comforts flee,
> Help of the helpless, oh, abide with me.
>
> I need Thy presence every passing hour;
> What but Thy grace can foil the tempter's pow'r?
> Who, like Thyself, my guide and stay can be?
> Through cloud and sunshine, Lord, abide with me.
>
> Hold Thou Thy cross before my closing eyes;
> Shine through the gloom and point me to the skies;
> Heav'n's morning breaks and earth's vain shadows flee;
> In life, in death, O Lord, abide with me.[2]

Lyrics have a way of settling our souls even in the most unsettling situations. My body was being triggered by past experiences of driving solo through fog with screaming babies in the backseat. Everything in me wanted to pull over and just wait it out, but I had no idea how long the gloom would remain. I knew the temperature was dropping and soon all the rain would be shifting into snow, and the best plan for me was to keep driving. So I took some deep breaths, slowed down, turned up my tunes, and invited Jesus into the moment with me.

Instead of trying to tackle the anxiety of this scary circumstance alone, I remembered that Jesus was *with* me. In the Message, Eugene Peterson paraphrases Paul's words from 1 Corinthians like this:

> We don't yet see things clearly. We're squinting in a fog, peering through a mist. But it won't be long before the weather clears and the sun shines bright! We'll see it all then, see it all as clearly as God sees us, knowing him directly just as he knows us! (1 Cor. 13:12)

As I drove through every curve, nearly blind to my surroundings, I knew I was not alone, and it made all the difference.

Our God Who Designs in Beauty and Dwells in Glory

At this point in the book of Exodus, God gave Moses very specific, detailed instructions on building the tabernacle, the elaborate tent that would symbolize God's presence among the Israelites. "Then have them make a sanctuary for me, and I will dwell among them. Make this tabernacle and all its furnishings exactly like the pattern I will show you" (Exod. 25:8–9).

Every moment of the Exodus narrative has been pointing to the reality that God's heartbeat is to dwell *with* Israel. He is not a far-off God who wants his people to do life on their own. He longs to be close so that we might all glean from the glory of his goodness.

God's design for the tabernacle was intentionally symbolic and included intricate plans for the ark of the covenant and the mercy seat, which was where God's glory would dwell inside the tent. The ark contained a jar of manna as a reminder of God's daily provision in the desert.[3] A beautiful curtain divided the tent's interior into two parts and veiled the most holy place, where the ark of the covenant was placed.[4] *Every material* that was used had significance and pointed to God's nature and transcendence in the midst of his broken people.

Like the tabernacle, we were created by the Master Designer with a specific design and purpose in mind. We each have the capacity for *creativity*, and God allows us to join him in cocreating, so that we might point back to his glory. He has gifted us each with the ability to reflect his image to the world in our own unique way. Emily Freeman writes, "I don't believe there is one great thing I was made to do in this world. I believe there is one great God I was made to glorify. And there will be many ways, even a million little ways, I will declare his glory with my life."[5]

> » In what ways do you think you were made to cocreate with God, our Master Designer? List some ideas.

The best part is that God wants to be part of the process. He didn't just tell the Israelites to build any kind of tabernacle; he made a plan that mirrored his *dwelling* in heaven.[6] Here we see a tangible expression of heaven meeting earth.

God also has a plan for us as his living tabernacles who roam the earth every single day. As Paul reminds us in Ephesians, "And in him you too are being built together to become a dwelling in which God lives by his Spirit" (Eph. 2:22).

To have some context for what this means today, we first must explore why the curtain created a visible separation within the tabernacle. God wants to be close to us, but sin is a barrier that separates us from him. The curtain was a visual image of the wall of sin between God and his people. We need a way to break down that barrier between us and God.

In the Old Testament the Israelites' only hope of forgiveness was through offering animal sacrifices. But the blood of the animals was only a temporary solution. So that the curtain divider would be torn down once and for all, God chose to send his Son, Jesus, to bring us back into relationship with him. When Jesus died, no more blood had to be shed, and the curtain was torn in half to show our redemption.

God also has a plan for us as his living tabernacles who roam the earth every single day.

The way the dots connect from the Exodus story to the New Testament is summarized in a striking comment Bono made in an interview with Eugene Peterson just a few years ago: "I have no problem with the Old Testament, I don't think God is a violent God, but I think the world is a violent place, and it does reflect that . . . and it's a terrifying thing, some of the Old Testament, but it is real and in a way I kind of prefer it to the airy fairy, where we don't get real."[7]

God's sacrifice in Jesus is his love letter to the world.

God loves us so deeply that he *gave* us the gift of Jesus as our Manna. He is the bridge back to our heavenly Father, who dwells with us in our everyday life.

We all have the choice, no matter what our background or story, no matter how far gone we might feel, to accept the love of our Maker, who knit us together.

Jesus is our *hidden Manna*, the One we have been longing for.[8]

Full Life Includes Both Peace and Pain

Entering a relationship with Jesus does not prevent us from feeling the whiplash from this world. In surrendering to God's best, hunting for the beauty in the mess, and unearthing the manna in every moment, *we will still feel pain.* Sadly, no one can put a bow on tragedy, loss, and disappointment, as we all know that darkness lurks around every corner.

Full life consists of both peace and pain. It is hard to have one without the other. We don't crave peace unless we feel pain. We don't know how to define pain unless we've had peace. They are in extreme opposition, yet they happen to coexist in this place that we call life here on earth. In the in-between places, in the middle of our stories, in the already and not yet. We especially get to taste the goodness when we feel the veil between heaven and earth thinning. For me personally this has been when people I love have left earth too soon and pain persists. These are times when what really matters is pushed to the forefront and everything else pales in comparison to what is happening right now.

Full life consists of both peace and pain. It is hard to have one without the other.

I've woken up to the reality of this when:

a dear friend's mom passed in a pedestrian accident in the heart of our town.

similar messages follow me around through books, music, and friends' words.

friends' marriages have crumbled due to affairs and addiction and been restored.

a young mom and faithful friend had to undergo a kidney transplant.

a healthy young father in our community developed a neurological disorder.

my children have lost their innocence as they have grown older.

a dear family friend suffered an aneurysm while on a treadmill.

friends send a text by the prompting of the Spirit that speaks right to my soul.

a local family experienced both a sudden heart attack and a drowning within months.

I've listened to the pastoral and prophetic voice of a random Uber driver.

my mentor headed to heaven before we got to finish our bantering conversations.

there has been both mourning and dancing and I've experienced God's glory.

When my eyes are open to see all that God is effortlessly revealing to me, I stand in awe.

When I wake up, I realize he is right here and has been all along.

The difference is that when we surrender to trusting Jesus and enter a relationship with him, recognizing him as the ultimate Manna in our life, we do find *peace.* Peace that shows up no matter what is happening or what we might feel that we are lacking. A peace from God that the Bible explains in Philippians, that appears in the fog and storms of life, that transcends all understanding and is beyond our brain's ability to grasp.

Rejoice in the Lord always. I will say it again: Rejoice! Let your gentleness be evident to all. *The Lord is near.* Do not be anxious about anything, but in every situation, by prayer and petition, with thanksgiving, present your requests to God. And the *peace* of God, which transcends all understanding, will guard your hearts and your minds in Christ Jesus. (Phil. 4:4–7, italics added)

Rejoice. Do not be anxious. Be thankful. This is where we all seem to fall short, right?

> » **How do you find yourself resisting God's peace**
> **when life brings unexpected circumstances?**

We do not always rejoice. We are at times anxious. Yet we can experience gratitude no matter the circumstances.

So we ask ourselves these tough questions, we search our soul, and we come to terms with our longing in a land that is loud and tries to offer us everything but leaves us starving apart from Jesus.

eighteen

A FEW YEARS AGO we spent a weekend up at Windy Gap, a Young Life camp nestled in a valley in the North Carolina mountains. It was just after dinner and all of camp was bustling with high school guys and girls who had spent a day running around, ziplining, and basking in the sun. The autumn leaves were hanging by a thread in every shade of gold, and my heart was full watching everyone untethered to time.

It was dark in our cabin because I was getting ready to head down to the dining hall and knew we had to have all the lights turned off for the next twenty minutes. On Saturday nights after the all-camp cross talk, guys and girls are given the opportunity to sit in silence under the stars and process life. I checked my phone for the time and my CaringBridge app had alerted me with an update. My heart sank because I knew what an update meant.

My friend Kristen Milligan was nearing the end of her decade-long battle with cancer, and for weeks I had been expecting to hear news that she had stepped into heaven.

About six months earlier I had driven up to visit Kristen for what I knew would probably be the last time. I remembered that one of my favorite singer-songwriter duos, Jenny & Tyler, were releasing a new album that day. So I turned on iTunes and listened to it the whole way up. The entire album is a prelude to the Easter story and a remembrance of all Jesus has done by his death and resurrection. Every lyric of the final song, "Kingdom of Heaven," brought tears to my eyes as I was thinking about Kristen's life here on earth coming to an end.

With my middle son in tow, I carried a gift basket inspired by Ann Voskamp's *One Thousand Gifts* up the winding staircase to Kristen's mountain house. We sat together and chatted about everything from the mountain view to nursing babies to the squirrel on the birdfeeder. We laughed and cried. Mourning and dancing. Somehow Kristen found the kingdom of heaven in her valley, which gives us all hope to find manna in our own valleys.

I noticed a *book* she had nearby titled *The Gift of Being Yourself* by David Benner. It was required reading for my master's program in counseling and I loved that she was reading it. Our time together was so precious to me, and I was amazed by the peace she felt in the midst of what loomed ahead for her family. She modeled a calming peace during a turbulent time that I will never forget. Over the past decade she had chosen, alongside her husband Deric, to create an organization called Inheritance of Hope, which cares for families like theirs in which a parent is terminally ill. Instead of letting the darkness win, Kristen chose to shed some light amid her own cancer battle and be manna for many others, and her legacy continues today through IOH.

So I glanced back down at my CaringBridge page and read that Kristen had indeed stepped into heaven. I felt equal parts relief and sadness wash over me in that moment. Within just a few seconds of reading that news, I heard the haunting sound of a guitar strumming. On the other side of our cabin wall, the camp musicians (who just happened to be Jenny & Tyler) were practicing for the night's song to be played at our gathering. You guessed it: "Kingdom of Heaven."

My manna.

I settled into the darkness of the room and hid underneath a blanket, allowing the couch to envelop me. Only the Lord could have orchestrated such *a soothing next five minutes for me*. He knew how much my heart was breaking and what that song meant to me the day I went to visit Kristen for the last time here on earth. It was one of those moments that I felt seen and known by a God who sometimes can feel so far off in times of loss and pain. When they had finished practicing, I headed down to camp. I looked up at the stars and rejoiced in the reality that Kristen was now with Jesus. The peace she had shown me was invading my own spirit, and I smiled through my tears.

God sees us. He knows just what we need when we don't even know it ourselves. He is our Manna, and he gives us glimpses of his glory in the form of manna made just for us, if we will only hunt for it! My greatest comfort that night was found not only in knowing that Kristen was healed, as she always told us she would be, even if it was in heaven, but in the tender presence of Jesus. Without even knowing it, Jenny & Tyler were manna for me in one of my heaviest moments as they sang those words over my soul. *When we use our gifts, we gift others* and point them to the One who made us and sees us and knows us and loves us.

Behold, the dwelling place of God is with man. He will dwell with them, and they will be his people, and God himself will be with them as their God. He will wipe away every tear from their eyes, and death shall be no more, neither shall there be mourning, nor crying, nor pain anymore, for the former things have passed away. And he who was seated on the throne said, "Behold, I am making all things new." (Rev. 21:3–5 ESV)

> » Have you ever had a moment in your life that could only be explained to have come from God himself? Take some time to pause and write some times down. Thank God for knowing you better than you know yourself and for knowing what you need. Keep a record of these times when you feel seen, known, and loved.

Living Fully in a Land of Longing

I have found that the most important part of living fully in a land of longing is being present enough to remember that *God is with us* and that we are not alone. It is our tendency many days to just go through the motions and do our best to survive this life.

But what if the reason that nothing in this world seems like enough is because it isn't? It never will be. We could spend the rest of our lives trying to find something that will fulfill us, and we will always come up empty. The truth is that all we really need in life is Jesus.

Moses and the Israelites left Mount Sinai, where they had learned all about what righteous living looks like. They had rebelled and they had been forgiven. They had built the tabernacle. God had renewed his covenant with them and they were about to continue their journey home.

What enabled them to keep going in faith was the realization that God had been with them all along. At this point they were more convinced than ever of *his presence*.

> » What if we were able to recognize God's nearness in the mundane of our everyday? What if we could find him in every detail? What if we hunted for the manna in every single moment?

The best part is, we can still have a laundry list of earthly desires and goals in mind to work toward, but the urgency to make it all happen ourselves and cover up the deeper ache begins to fade when we start to believe in what really matters in life and what fulfills us. When we begin that sweet surrender, somehow our own strivings start to lose their grip on us. We gain perspective and realize that it isn't so much about how hard we hustle, but it is more about how we rest and rely on the One who holds the stars in the sky and calls them each by name.[9]

Sometimes it's not even our own longings that affect us but the longings of those we love. We ache as others ache.

Amid all the heaviness this world brings, we can see the loving hand of God threaded throughout each story, and his provision becomes evident. The understanding that he can transcend the framework of time gives us a newfound willingness to trust him in what we cannot see ahead. We still may think we know what is best, but at the end of the day we can come to a place of surrender in the depths of our souls. Every morning when we wake up, when our old nature tries to take over, we can pray for courage to release control back into the hands of our Maker and Creator, who really does know best.

So this raises the question: *Are we meant to simply deny our greatest longings and gloss over the emotions that follow?* I argue that we are not. We were made by a loving Maker who knit us together in our mother's womb. In his great and glorious plan, nothing is wasted.

Whenever I'm having a dark day, I play a song by my friend Ellie Holcomb called "Don't Forget His Love," which is based on Psalm 108. As I let her words of hope and rescue seep deeply into my soul, they breathe fresh life back into my bones.

When truth washes over us, hope halts our heart. We stop going down that spiral of despair and we remember all God has done. *Friends and family speak truth* to remind us of this. God himself breathes light into our darkness if we will only allow him to enter the place where we dwell.

We remember that God sees us, he is near, and he will never, ever leave us![10]

We have seen the brokenness in our own life and in the lives of others and how it all emerges over the years. We have a new lens now and see that God's plan and provision are far greater than anything we can dream up or imagine. At the end of the day we know that until we arrive in heaven, we will be left wanting by the next thing we long for. But we choose to keep going, discovering the manna in our midst in every season we encounter and finding contentment within the longing.

So this is where the hunt continues.

We open our eyes, we discover the beauty in the mess, and we find the manna in every moment. We become *fully present* and mindful of what is good right here, right now with every breath.

This is how we live in a land of longing while we await heaven and all that is to come.

Deliverance

There are countless ways we see God meet the Israelites in their lost identity during slavery, in their wandering forgetfulness, and even in their ungrateful disobedience. Exodus is a relevant narrative that points to the greatest love story and rescue in all of history. We all have our own individual narratives within God's great narrative. People in any season can experience the nearness of God, who meets us right where we are in our wandering and yearning. Hebrews says:

> Therefore, since we are surrounded by such a great cloud of witnesses, let us throw off everything that hinders and the sin that so easily entangles. And let us run with perseverance the race marked out for us, fixing our eyes on Jesus, the pioneer and perfecter of faith. For the joy set before him he endured the cross, scorning its shame, and sat down at the right hand of the throne of God. Consider him who endured such opposition from sinners, so that you will not grow weary and lose heart. (Heb. 12:1–3)

Our reality might feel far from that most days, yet we can experience more satisfaction than we ever realized was possible. Ann Voskamp says, "We give thanks to God not because of how we feel, but because of who He is."[11] We can feel content in the sense that we are given just enough, if not more than we need, in every waking moment each day. It comes in odd forms some days, but every time we feel seen by God we can find ourselves whispering "manna."

Every single one of these manna moments, though they may seem small, ends up bringing a smile to my face and a swelling in my heart. They are reminders that our God loves us deeply. He knows us so well that he meets us right where we are. He anticipates what we need and when and how. Sometimes he even prompts the hearts of other people to supply our need in a more concrete way. He allows us as his cocreators to be the hands and feet of his body. He notices our

It comes in odd forms some days, but every time we feel seen by God we can find ourselves whispering "manna."

heartache and refuses to let us sit and wallow in the pain. He longs to make himself known to us, and sometimes if we can slow down, *we see him.* We will be stunned by the gifts and awed by his creativity and ability to make us laugh and cry simultaneously. We will see his hand in the highlights and low valleys of life. We will experience him richly when nothing else lasts and the ways of this world leave us wanting. Just as the Israelites were delivered, we can cry, "Deliver me, O God! Rescue me and keep me from taking back the reins of my life."

So maybe the way of full life here on earth isn't so much about reaching the promised land as it is about finding the One who made you and me and is right here with us on the journey. May we rest in knowing he is near and we have all we need with his *Holy Spirit* dwelling in us. His presence is enough.

For this reason I bow my knees before the Father, from whom every family in heaven and on earth takes its name. I pray that, according to the riches of his glory, he may grant that you may be strengthened in your inner being with power through his Spirit, and that Christ may dwell in your hearts through faith, as you are being rooted and grounded in love. I pray that you may have the power to comprehend, with all the saints, what is the breadth and length and height and depth, and to know the love of Christ that surpasses knowledge, so that you may be filled with all the fullness of God. (Eph. 3:14–19 NRSV)

May we be like the birds,
resting in the knowledge that our help comes from the Lord.

May we take hold of the Bread of Life,
our ultimate Provider and Manna.

May we shift our eyes from our lack and
find our satisfaction in the presence of Jesus.

Amen.

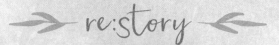

re:story

1. How do you feel about God choosing to dwell among the Israelites and with us today? Is it more comforting or alarming to you? Take some time to write about why.

2. What does it look like daily for you to abide and enjoy the presence of Jesus? When and where have you felt his presence lately? What does it stir up in you?

3. What helps you to fix your eyes on Jesus and trust God when life gets hard? What are some areas where God is inviting you to let him enter in more?

4. What are you thankful for even during your hard seasons? List them and write about why and how you can be grateful anyway.

5. What does it look like for you personally to live life fully in a land of longing? How have you found yourself hunting for manna in the midst of this journey?

re:sound

"Lighten Our Darkness" by Greg LaFollette

"We draw people to Christ not by loudly discrediting what they believe, by telling them how wrong they are and how right we are, but by showing them a light that is so lovely that they want with all their hearts to know the source of it."

—Madeleine L'Engle

epilogue

Manna Makers

I know what it is to be in need, and I know what it is to
have plenty. I have learned the secret of being content
in any and every situation, whether well fed or hungry,
whether living in plenty or in want.

Philippians 4:12

WHEN WE SEARCH for manna in our life, we can see God's
hand, whether we are in want or plenty.

As we survey the rugged landscape we have covered in
this narrative journey through Exodus, it is nearly impossible
to ignore God's provision in the lives of the Israelites. We
have taken intentional time to look back, be still, and scan
the horizon. We have stepped back into the garden of Eden,
weighed the beauty and pain of the in-between, and glimpsed
the glory of heaven.

As we have considered every story, we have seen a common thread that points to God's grander narrative that we are all swept up in. Naming our humanity has reminded us of our brokenness and our inability to restore ourselves on our own. We have found our Rescuer—Jesus, God's ultimate Manna, who loves us with such abundance there can't help but be overflow. Eugene Peterson puts it like this in his vibrant paraphrase from 2 Corinthians:

When we search for manna in our life, we can see God's hand, whether we are in want or plenty.

God can pour on the blessings in astonishing ways so that you're ready for anything and everything, more than just ready to do what needs to be done. As one psalmist puts it,

He throws caution to the winds,
   giving to the needy in reckless abandon.
His right-living, right-giving ways
   never run out, never wear out.

This most generous God who gives seed to the farmer that becomes bread for your meals is more than extravagant with you. He gives you something you can then give away, which grows into full-formed lives, robust in God, wealthy in every way, so that you can be generous in every way, producing with us great praise to God. (2 Cor. 9:8–11 Message)

When we live believing the truth that we already have all we need in Christ, we can love others as we were created to do. We become more able to extend God's grace and love to ourselves, and it naturally overflows onto others. Loving the people God puts in our path shifts from being the greatest command to the greatest gift. This kind of love helps us remember the rescue we so desperately needed in Jesus's death and resurrection on the cross.

> » After walking through this narrative experience
> what have you come to learn about God? About
> yourself and your story? about others? What
> practices do you want to adopt as you close this
> chapter?

The week I wrote these final words, I headed up to a friend's place in the mountains to finish the manuscript for this book. It was the week before Christmas, and this generous family who was sharing their cottage had a carload of gifts to be delivered to orphans at a local children's home. As my friend helped me load up all the gifts, I found myself in tears as I considered the hearts of these children in need. The next day I drove up the winding path to the home and entered the old stone-laced property to drop off the gifts.

The director of the center met me at the front door. She had kind eyes. She helped me unload each bag and we put each child's gifts under the tree, which had been bare when I arrived. She thanked me for the delivery as she shared the stories of a few kids who had deep wounds from sexual abuse or abandonment. As I drove away, I looked in the rearview mirror, imagining what Christmas morning would be like for these kids this year because of my friend's generosity. Tears started to stream down my face as I realized the difference this joyous extension of manna would make for these precious children.

We have so much to offer a world that dwells in this land of longing.

When we hear that small voice stirring in our spirits to extend love or grace to someone else, we tend to silence it as quickly as it speaks. We fight through cobwebs of doubt, telling ourselves that we are too busy or that we don't really have the bandwidth to give more than we already do. Our culture of entitlement preaches self-sufficiency, so we see those in need (ourselves included) as weak, and our default mind-set is to expect them to buck up. It sounds harsh, but at times it's the way we operate. This is the direct opposite of how Jesus calls us to live. He is whispering gently, *Be manna makers.*

When I signed the contract for this book, I was reluctant at first. I knew the Lord was calling me to write and share the hope that I had found with this metaphor of manna, but it just felt too daunting and hard. I honestly didn't think I was qualified or had what it takes to do it. Can you hear echoes of Moses in my doubting? Just as God spoke to Moses at the burning bush, he spoke in the depths of my heart, reminding me that he would give me what I needed to see this project to completion.

I knew I was going to need a team of people to serve as my backbone of support. I needed my own Miriam, Aaron, Zipporah, Jethro, and army of Israelites to go with me. I decided to gather some of my friends and ask them to specifically pray for me during this time. One morning I woke up and felt like the Lord had given me a name for this group of fifty women. I call them my "manna makers" because through each season of my story they have each shown love by extending manna in unique ways. They have used the gifts God gave them to show me light in my dark. When I couldn't remember—or when doubts smothered me—they reminded me that God is enough, no matter what circumstances I am battling on any given day. They have been my people and I have been theirs. Remember, we were all made differently and have unique gifts from God. Not one of us was made exactly alike, which is what makes this world vibrant and full of adventure. Maybe you love through listening. Maybe you love through creating. Maybe you love through speaking. Maybe you love through providing. Maybe you love through planning. We all *get* to love.

No matter what, God has given you the ability to shed some light in the dark places—because if he has a grip on your life, he is determined to use you and the way you move in the world to bring him glory. Jesus charges us with this in Matthew 5:16, where he says, "Let your light shine before others, so that they may see your good works and give glory to your Father who is in heaven" (ESV).

I think another way of saying this is that we are called to be *manna makers.* Just as Jesus has come to give us life by his presence, we can be an extension of him to others. Since God has come to dwell among us, we get the benefit of letting his love and light flow out of us in hopes that others might taste and see his goodness too. He leads us when we draw near.

What a delight it is to walk in the wonder of both receiving manna and giving manna!

So when you don't feel like you have what it takes to love other people, remember that you are not alone. God is inviting you to join him on this journey of loving his children. As Peter writes, "Each of you should use whatever gift you have received to serve others, as faithful stewards of God's grace in its various forms" (1 Pet. 4:10).

The way I love people is most likely going to look different from the way you love people. One of my favorite books is

written by a feisty older woman named Jill Briscoe. She wrote
a book with the title *Here I Am, Lord . . . Send Somebody Else,*
which is a play on Isaiah 6:8. I laugh every time I read the title
because it's so *me!* It's so Moses. I wonder, is it also so *you?*
Do you believe that God can help you be a manna maker in
the lives of your family, friends, neighbors, coworkers, and
even strangers?

One thing that makes me support the resurgence of the Enneagram in our culture today is that it points us to the reality
that we are to celebrate how we were all made *differently.* It
reminds us that the way we operate in the world is not an accident, but is actually handcrafted by a God whose whole strat-
egy is to love the world in such a way that any person who does
not know him is without excuse.[1] We are all image-bearers,
uniquely designed to help point like arrows back to our Creator by the way we live our life. This is not 1950s Pleasantville
living where we are all supposed to fit into a mold and live life
according to formulaic traditional roles; this is a modern-day
millennial "you do you" mind-set turned on its head. We get
the freeing gift of living out our purpose and utilizing the talents
that God gave us in our everyday. The whole world benefits
when we are not just trying to be like someone else.

The reality is though, that God is ultimately able to woo
us without using other people. But I bet if I were to sit down
with the people in your life who have loved you well up to this
point, they would say what a gift and honor it has been for
them to be a part of your story. What a gift it is to see someone *find their identity* again when they are reminded that
they have a God who loves them. God allows us to be a part
of reminding each other what is true when we forget. We are
given relationships that point to him.

I love the part in the Gospel of Luke when Jesus and his disciples are heading to Jerusalem:

Right at the crest, where Mount Olives begins its descent, the whole crowd of disciples burst into enthusiastic praise over all the mighty works they had witnessed:

> Blessed is he who comes,
>   the king in God's name!
> All's well in heaven!
>   Glory in the high places!

Some Pharisees from the crowd told him, "Teacher, get your disciples under control!"

But he said, "If they kept quiet, the stones would do it for them, shouting praise." (Luke 19:37–40 Message)

What a humbling reminder that God can reveal his goodness to the world without us. Yet he gives us the invitation to have a front-row seat in watching others catch a glimpse of his glory. He didn't have to include us.

As I look back over the last few decades of my life, I am blown away by the people who have loved me and pointed me back to Jesus. I instantly think of my mentors in various seasons of my life like Bobbi, Georgia, Holly, Jenn, Karen, Mark, Paula, Sande, Terry, and Wanda. I would not be who I am today without them. We need each other in the practical mundane and the tragic unexpected. We need people to lean on. We need *manna makers* in our life.

> » Who comes to mind as your manna makers? Who has poured into you over the years?

I've needed these tangible forms of manna too:

parents and in-laws who have believed in me and my
    husband and invested in our family,
friends who bring meals when life happens and I need a
    hand,
texts with links to music or Scripture that fill me up,
shoulders to cry on when I have no words just tears,
checks that show up in our mailbox when a bill is almost
    due,
a stranger's kind smile as they hold the door for my wild
    crew,
our two dogs that we found on a local greenway and
    rescued,
a home with more than we could have dreamed up,
a cozy new coffee shop to write these words comfortably,
gatherings of Spirit-led men and women who remind me
    who I am and to keep going,
and so much more.

I wonder where the manna is overflowing in your life? You
might be blown away when you put on your new lens to hunt
it. Once we wake up, it's everywhere!

As we close our time together, may we use these verses
from Isaiah as a reminder that God goes before us and makes
a way where there seems to be no way:

> If you are generous with the hungry
>   and start giving yourselves to the down-and-out,
> Your lives will begin to glow in the darkness,
>   your shadowed lives will be bathed in sunlight.

I will always show you where to go.
I'll give you a full life in the emptiest of places—
firm muscles, strong bones.
You'll be like a well-watered garden,
a gurgling spring that never runs dry.
You'll use the old rubble of past lives to build anew,
rebuild the foundations from out of your past.
You'll be known as those who can fix anything,
restore old ruins, rebuild and renovate,
make the community livable again. (Isa. 58:10–12
Message)

Our Maker, who is our ultimate Manna, is in the business of feeding our souls and re-storying our lives in a way that only he can. "For even the Son of Man did not come to be served, but to serve, and to give his life as a ransom for many" (Mark 10:45). He is the Sower who make the seeds grow and brings flowers from thorny cactuses that spring up in the desert.

We have an opportunity once we wake up to find freedom, to walk confidently in the ways of our Maker. Whether we are in want or plenty, may we have fresh eyes to see ourselves and others as manna makers, not for our own glory but for God's. May we bloom in desert places. Amen.

Our Maker, who is our ultimate Manna, is in the business of feeding our souls and re-storying our lives in a way that only he can.

re:story

1. Who have been the manna makers in your life over the years?

2. How was their love manna for you and/or others?

3. Where do you feel God is calling you to be a manna maker in your own life?

4. What keeps you from sharing the manna you are created to share?

5. How can you practically be manna for others during this season in your life?

re:sound

"Help Me to Give" by You Me & the Bread

May we Bloom in the desert Places.

-MEREDITH McDANIEL

true cotton

Manna makers, may we go in peace together, letting these soothing words wash over our souls as a manna benediction from one of my favorite singer-songwriters, John Lucas. May we rest in seeing that our Maker lovingly crafts our story by his grace and "paints beauty with time."

"Time"

My heart has known the winters
And my feet have known the snow
But mine eyes have seen the glory
Of a seed begin to grow

There is a time to uproot, darling
But most days just hold on tight
For there's a time for darkness, honey
But dawn will always beat the night

Sometimes death will come calling
When you've been good and warned
And other times its cold hands will cradle
Dreams yet to be born

There is a time to dance on sorrow
And a time to kiss her cheek
There is a time to mourn in silence
But justice aches to hear you speak

And I don't know the end, or tomorrow's story
But I have found the one who gives me rest
And I will make my bed in His promises
For He holds true when nothing's left . . . When
    nothing's left

There is a time when laughter will echo
Through your halls of peace

But war is known to change your locks
And carry off the family keys
There is a time for healing and pain
A time for drought and a time for rain
There is a time for everything
Until we crown the risen King . . . Until we crown the
    risen King

And I don't know the end, or tomorrow's story
But I have found the one who gives me rest
And I will make my bed in His promises
For He holds true when nothing's left . . . When
    nothing's left

So crown Him in your mourning
And crown Him in your laughter
And crown Him when it all turns dark
Crown Him when you bury
And crown Him when you marry
And crown Him when your faith finds a spark

Crown Him for He's faithful
And crown Him for He's worthy
And crown Him for He is good
Crown Him for His promises
Cut through the blindness
Of children that have barely understood

The beauty that has come
And the beauty yet to come
And the beauty that is yours and that is mine
And that death produces life
And that we are made alive
By the King who paints beauty with time
By the King who paints beauty with time
By the King who paints beauty with time

And I don't know the end, or tomorrow's story
But I have found the one who gives me rest
And I will make my bed in His promises
For He holds true when nothing's left . . . When
nothing's left

acknowledgments

THIS BOOK WOULD NOT be in your hands if it was not for Jesus, our Manna, and all the *manna makers* in my life.

Writing the words tucked within these pages has been the most refining and raw experience of my lifetime to date. I am utterly grateful for the team of people who have come alongside me during this process when I wanted to give up and when self-doubt shouted louder than God's whispers.

All of these men and women have shared their stories with me in their own unique ways and have given me the courage to be vulnerable in hopes that some light would be shed in the darkness.

Ben, thank you for always balancing out my dark with your light and for wrangling our crew when I was on a deadline. Thank you for laying down your life for so many to show us all that our stories are redeemable.

Grady, Judah, and Ellis, thank you for giving me the grace to get away a few times this year to write. Thank you for singing, drawing, writing, snuggling, and constantly reminding me that our primary relationships are the greatest form of manna we are given here on earth, reflecting Jesus.

Mom, Dad, Nana, and Mac, thank you for believing in me and investing in our family for the long haul. We could not manage all our chaos without your constant support and love for us and our little people. Laurie and Jonathan, Madeline and Ryan, Scottie and Marshall, Shane and Courtney, thanks for being my brothers and sisters who always cheer me on endlessly.

To all my grandparents, aunts and uncles, and cousins near and far, thank you for wrapping your loving arms around me and always being faithful reminders of the bonds and memories a family provides.

Emily, thank you for creating space for my soul to breathe and modeling for me what it looks like to do my next right thing in love. I would not be holding this book in my hands without you and your words of encouragement over the past five years. You have been manna for me. Thank you for building an "artist bench" for me to join you and some kindred spirits early on. Thank you for writing the most heart-swelling foreword, friend.

Endorsers, thank you for taking your valuable time to read, review, and offer up such gracious words and for backing this book. I am honored.

Allume women, who made space for me at your table: Logan, Reeve, Kendra, Myquillyn, Sarah, Kristen, Shannan, Amber, Amena, and Ruth, thank you for showing me authors are people too, through laughter and tears.

To my editor Kelsey Bowen and my whole publishing team at Revell, thank you for latching on to this metaphor of manna and letting it unfold in God's perfect time. Your ability to see the vision for this book is why it exists today. Thank you to Amy, Eileen, and Gayle for every tiny detail that has made a big difference, from the cover to every comma.

Thanks to my friend Arin Guthe of True Cotton Art for capturing my vision of cacti blooming in a desert that tugs our heart toward the promised land. Thank you to my friend Michelle Shott for capturing some calm in my headshot while our kids ran wild by the lake on the edge of your property.

My Lake Forest Davidson church family, thank you for "loving people as they discover and live out their role in God's story" and for providing a deeply rooted place for our town to gather and be reminded of the *manna in our midst*, no matter where we are in our journey. Thank you for your humility and the ways you love others so deeply and encourage all who come around to share in their gifts by looking up and looking around.

You, Me, and the Bread: thank you for providing a refreshing soundtrack for the rounds and rounds of edits it took to finally finish well.

Local friends and those from afar, thank you for being my people and for loving me as I am. There are too many of you to list, but thank each of you for praying me through all these years. Special thanks for my Davidson Prayer Triad, Revells in the Queen City, and Voxey Ladies. Love you dearly.

Kristin Leathers, Deric Milligan, Diane Smith, and Molly Warner, thank you for letting me share your stories with vulnerability and joy.

Young Life, Gordon-Conwell, Hope*writers, Inheritance of Hope, Rabbit Room, and The Breath and the Clay, thank you for being people who reveal Jesus and raise up disciples who point to our creative Creator. It is through your missions that artists, writers, musicians, and friends *make*.

Thank you, Ama, Ashley Abramson, Fil Anderson, Lucretia Berry, Hailey Brown, John Campbell, Cashes, Mark Christy, Emily Dean, Flakes, Gallaghers, Geers, Gibbs, Glasses, Sande Griebner, Guions, Hills, Jentz, Hope Kemp, Erika Knox, Sierra MacFarlane, Elizabeth Maxon, Martha Metzler, Moriseys, Karen Overly, KJ Ramsey, Mary Mac Brookins, Seymour Sisters, Shotts, Wagenhausers, Leigh Whitaker, Tiffany Wilkinson, Hollins Worsley, Worsleys, and Zuiderveens, for believing in this project and offering up your prayers and space for me over the years.

Thanks to Dr. Gwenfair Adams, Dr. Dan Allender, Dr. Gregg Blanton, Dr. Larry Crabb, Dr. Jennifer Thomas, Dr. Christine Palmer, and Dr. Curt Thompson, for your wisdom and influence on my lifelong learning.

SheReadsTruth, IF:Gathering, Bible Project, and every author, artist, musician, and poet referenced in this book and beyond, thank you for being a resource to me by offering your gifts to shine in this world.

To you, my brave reader, thank you for being willing to let me take your hand as together we unearthed manna in our story. May we all take what we have found and share it with the world, in both want and plenty.

re:story resources

National

American Association of Christian Counselors Connect

Christian Association for Psychological Studies Directory

Good Therapy

Inheritance of Hope

National Domestic Violence Hotline

National Eating Disorders Association

National Suicide Prevention Lifeline (1-800-273-TALK)

Psychology Today

SAMHSA Treatment Locator, https://findtreatment.samhsa.gov/

Regional

Allender Center

Barnabas Center

CareNet Counseling

Cornerstone Counseling Center

Davidson Lifeline

Grandfather Mountain Children's Home

Milk + Honey Counseling

Sanctuary Counseling Group

Southeast Psych

notes

Prologue

1. Ian Cron and Suzanne Stabile, *The Road Back to You: An Enneagram Journey to Self-Discovery* (Downers Grove, IL: InterVarsity, 2016), 22.

2. "What Is the Enneagram?" The Narrative Enneagram, https://www.enneagramworldwide.com/the-enneagram/.

3. Dan Allender, *To Be Told: God Invites You to Coauthor Your Story* (Colorado Springs: Waterbrook, 2005), 5.

4. R. Alan Cole, *Exodus*, Tyndale Old Testament Commentaries (Downers Grove, IL: InterVarsity, 2008), 139.

Deep Groans

1. Fil Anderson, *Running on Empty: Contemplative Spirituality for Over-achievers* (Colorado Springs: Waterbrook, 2005).

2. C. S. Lewis, *The Problem of Pain* (New York: HarperCollins, 2001), 91.

3. Exodus 1:8–11.

4. *Merriam-Webster*, s.v. "want," https://www.merriam-webster.com/dictionary/want.

5. Genesis 2:8–9.

6. Genesis 2:16–17.

7. Genesis 3:4–5.

8. Larry Crabb, *Shattered Dreams: God's Unexpected Path to Joy* (Colorado Springs: Waterbrook, 2010), 116.

9. Exodus 3:7–8.

10. A term coined by St. John of the Cross in his poem by the same name.

Brick + Mortar

1. J. Alec Motyer, *The Message of Exodus: The Days of Our Pilgrimage* (Downers Grove, IL: InterVarsity, 2005), 28.

2. Allender, *To Be Told*, 44.

3. Suzanne Stabile, *The Path Between Us: An Enneagram Journey to Healthy Relationships* (Downers Grove, IL: InterVarsity, 2018), 3.

4. Exodus 33:14.

5. John 10:10; Matthew 11:28–30.

6. 1 Corinthians 15:58.

7. Julia Cameron, *The Artist's Way* (New York: Penguin Random House, 2016), 2.

Mighty Hand

1. Ann Voskamp, *The Broken Way: A Daring Path to the Abundant Life* (Grand Rapids: Zondervan, 2016), 53.

2. Jess Connolly and Hayley Morgan, *Wild and Free: A Hope-Filled Anthem for the Woman Who Feels She Is Both Too Much and Never Enough* (Grand Rapids: Zondervan, 2016).

3. Exodus 4:10–13.

4. Exodus 7:6–13.

5. Exodus 8–10.

6. Exodus 12:13.

7. Exodus 12:29–30.

8. Exodus 12:37–39.

9. Alastair J. Roberts and Andrew Wilson, *Echoes of Exodus: Tracing the Themes of Redemption through Scripture* (Wheaton: Crossway, 2018), 43.

10. Voskamp, *The Broken Way*, 53.

Tribe by Tribe

1. Exodus 12:40.

2. Elaine Aron, *The Highly Sensitive Person: How to Thrive When the World Overwhelms You* (New York: Broadway, 1997).

3. Romans 12:2.

4. Frederick Buechner, *Wishful Thinking: A Seeker's ABC* (New York: HarperOne, 1973), 95.

5. Isaiah 54:17.

6. Emily P. Freeman, *A Million Little Ways: Uncover the Art You Were Made to Live* (Grand Rapids: Revell, 2014), 21.

Fire + Cloud

1. https://usroute89.com.
2. Wendell Berry, "1994: III," in *A Timbered Choir: The Sabbath Poems* (Berkeley: Counterpoint, 1991), 178.
3. Douglas K. Stuart, *Exodus*, New American Standard Commentary (Nashville: B&H, 2006), 323.
4. Motyer, *Message of Exodus*, 169.
5. Thomas Merton, *New Seeds of Contemplation* (New York: New Directions, 1949), 258.
6. Walter Brueggemann, *Exodus*, The New Interpreter's Bible Commentary (Nashville: Abingdon, 1994), 789.

Dry Ground

1. Motyer, *Message of Exodus*, 179.
2. Harvard Health Publishing, "Understanding the Stress Response," March 2011, https://www.health.harvard.edu/staying-healthy/understanding-the-stress-response, updated May 1, 2018.
3. Brueggemann, *Exodus*, 793.
4. J. A. Brefczynski-Lewis et al., *Proceedings of the National Academy of Sciences of the United States of America* 104 (27): 11483–88.
5. Marie-Nathalie Beaudoin and Jeffrey Zimmerman, "Narrative Therapy and Interpersonal Neurobiology: Revisiting Classic Practices, Developing New Emphases," *Journal of Systemic Therapies* 30, no. 1 (2011): 2, https://theclinician.files.wordpress.com/2012/06/narrative-therapy-and-interpersonal-neurobiology.pdf.
6. Exodus 14:16.
7. Exodus 14:19–20.
8. Exodus 14:31.
9. Annie F. Downs, "When the Most Wonderful Time of the Year Is Messy," (in)courage, December 2, 2016, https://www.incourage.me/2016/12/wonderful-time-year-messy.html.
10. Sue Monk Kidd, *When the Heart Waits: Spiritual Direction for Life's Sacred Questions* (San Francisco: HarperCollins, 1990), 111.
11. Heather Kelly, "Apple's Screen Time Feature Proves You're Addicted to Your iPhone," CNN Business, June 25, 2018, https://money.cnn.com/2018/06/25/technology/iphone-screen-time-test/index.html.
12. T. Desmond Alexander, *Exodus*, Teach the Text Commentary Series (Grand Rapids: Baker Books, 2016), 16.
13. Sally Lloyd-Jones, *Thoughts to Make Your Heart Sing* (Grand Rapids: Zonderkidz, 2012).

Bread + Water

1. Exodus 15:25–26.
2. Exodus 16:31.
3. Exodus 16:20.
4. Exodus 16:35.

Etched in Stone

1. Exodus 17:1–7.
2. Exodus 17:8–16.
3. Exodus 18:1–27.
4. Motyer, *Message of Exodus*, 187.
5. Motyer, *Message of Exodus*, 191.
6. Motyer, *Message of Exodus*, 192.
7. Exodus 20:18–21.
8. Romans 3:23.
9. 2 Corinthians 12:9–11.
10. Curt Thompson, *The Soul of Shame: Retelling the Stories We Believe about Ourselves* (Downers Grove, IL: InterVarsity, 2015), 36.
11. Roberts and Wilson, *Echoes of Exodus*, 51.
12. Roberts and Wilson, *Echoes of Exodus*, 47.
13. Henry Cloud and John Townsend, *Boundaries Books*, https://www.boundariesbooks.com.
14. *The Heart of Man*, directed by Eric Esau, (2017; Unearthed Pictures, 2017), DVD.
15. 1 Peter 5:8.
16. Larry Crabb, *When God's Way Makes No Sense* (Grand Rapids: Baker Books, 2018), 80.
17. Romans 6:23.
18. Exodus 32:1–20.

Dwelling Place

1. Simona Chitescu Weik, "Coming Home to Our Bodies," The Allender Center blog, December 17, 2018, https://theallendercenter.org/2018/12/coming-home-to-our-bodies/, italics in original.
2. Henry Francis Lyte, "Abide with Me," 1847, stanzas 1, 3, and 5.
3. Exodus 16:32–34.
4. Exodus 25–26.
5. Freeman, *A Million Little Ways*, 40.
6. Hebrews 8:5.

7. "Bono & Eugene Peterson: The Psalms," YouTube video, 18:15, posted by Fuller Studio on April 26, 2016, https://www.youtube.com/watch?v=-l40S5e90KY.

8. Revelation 2:17.

9. Isaiah 40:26.

10. Deuteronomy 31:6.

11. Ann Voskamp, Twitter post, November 25, 2013, https://twitter.com/annvoskamp/status/405054684622106624.

Epilogue

1. Romans 1:20.

Meredith McDaniel is a licensed professional counselor and owner of her private practice Milk + Honey. A graduate of Gordon-Conwell Theological Seminary, she has also served on staff with Young Life and as the Lead Counselor with Inheritance of Hope. Meredith says she feels called to sit with and listen to the stories of women and men, helping them discover who they are and experience life more fully. She enjoys entering into the quieter places of people's lives in a safe setting to offer hope and help others taste of the land of milk + honey. She and her husband, Ben, have three young children and live in a small town near Charlotte, North Carolina.

Connect with
Meredith

MeredithMcDaniel.com

Meredith_McDaniel
MeredithMcDanielWriter
MereMcDaniel

MILK + HONEY
counseling

Meredith has vast experience working in a variety of settings with adolescents and women over the past fifteen years with Young Life and Inheritance of Hope. She has a passion to help both individuals and couples discover who they are and live the full life they were intended to live. Offering sessions both locally and from afar in her private practice.

For more information and narrative resources:

MILKANDHONEYCOUNSELING.COM